For All Those Who Dream Of Better Times & Better Places.

JAMES VAN HISE writes about film, television and comic book history. He has written numerous books on these subjects, including BATMANIA, TREK: THE NEXT GENERATION, THE TREK CREW BOOK, STEPHEN KING & CLIVE BARKER: THE ILLUSTRATED GUIDE TO THE MASTERS OF THE MACABRE and HOW TO DRAW ART FOR COMIC BOOKS: LESSONS FROM THE MASTERS. He is the publisher of MIDNIGHT GRAFFITI, in which he has run previously unpublished stories by Stephen King and Harlan Ellison. Van Hise resides in San Diego along with his wife, horses and various other animals.

Introduction

"When Lighting Struck the Same Place Twice"

It doesn't seem that long ago that I was among many other STAR TREK fans back in the Seventies hoping that the TV show would be revived some how. The original show. The one with Kirk and Spock. Only die-hard fans believed it was possible. After all, once a TV show was canceled it was on to rerun heaven with no chance of any sort of celluloid reincarnation. It just wasn't done. Even Gene Roddenberry didn't really think it would ever happen. The STAR TREK animated series of 1973 was just a part of a brief fad of that time which saw a brief cartoon show based on THE ADDAMS FAMILY television show and a LOST IN SPACE animated one-shot. But they were little more than blips on the creative horizon.

FLASH FORWARD 20 YEARS

Now in 1993 there have been six STAR TREK feature films featuring the original cast and two television series revivals—both spin-offs of the original universe dreamed by Gene Roddenberry in 1964 and finally given series life in 1966.

In 1973 no one, but no one, would have seriously believed that it would ever some to pass. From the 79 episodes of a defunct TV series have bloomed off-shoots which have surpassed the original in series longevity. STAR TREK—THE NEXT GENERATION is now 150 episodes strong, a success rate rarely equaled and even more rarely surpassed. Ordinarily only sitcoms manage to last so long, particularly at a time when the one-hour dramatic series are in a ratings slide.

When THE NEXT GENERATION was introduced in 1987, it was thought that it would appeal primarily to long time STAR TREK fans. But what has happened is that new fans have been attracted by the series so that people who never gave Kirk, Spock and McCoy the time of day have been attracted by Picard, Riker and Data. But it took some time.

THE NEXT GENERATION did fairly well in its first season but initially the ratings dropped markedly during reruns, meaning that people who'd seen an episode already weren't interested enough to watch it a second time. This has changed over the years as the characters have become established and the torch has clearly been passed between the original STAR TREK performers to the NEXT GENERATION. Patrick Stewart, Brent Spiner, Jonathan Frakes and the others have now appeared in more STAR TREK stories than the original TREK performers and this has an its inevitable effect.

THE NEXT GENERATION has become the STAR TREK standard bearer. These are the characters that the fans want to know more about.

In 1987 Pocket Books had a hard time finding writers willing to tackle NEXT GENERATION novels. Authors wanted to write about Trek Classic and Pocket had to tell them that they could do that only after writing a NEXT GENERATION novel first. The new series was on the air every week creating a new market to be filled and Pocket recognized this. NEXT GENERATION novels now are coming out with increased frequency, including hard covers by people like Peter David.

The crew of the Enterprise 1701-D have become what STAR TREK means to many, and perhaps a majority, of viewers today. Six years of adventures have given these characters a history and a depth which was, of course, missing in the first season. In fact we know a lot more about Picard than we've ever learned about Captain Kirk. And fans want more.

This book examines all of the crew members (including those who came and went, but nonetheless left their mark), including profiles of the actors who give life to the words of many writers.

THE NEXT GENERATION now is STAR TREK. When DEEP SPACE NINE was launched, it was spun off from NEXT GENERATION and takes place in that time frame, not the time frame of the adventures of Kirk and Spock. What seemed to some like a long shot has become the new tradition. Trek Classic has become old STAR TREK while the NEXT GENERATION has become the new future of the Enterprise and its crew.

Gene Roddenberry, deceased creator of Star Trek, surrounded by his two captains, Picard and Shatner.

Patrick Stewart- Headshot at the Sirtis/Lampert wedding.
Photo: © 1993 Ortega/Ron Galella Ltd.

CHAPTER 1

CAPTAIN JEAN-LUC PICARD

by Michael L. Ruff, Alex Burleson and David Gardner

Jean-Luc Picard was born July 13, 2305 in Labarre, France to Maurice and Evette Picard. His mother's maiden name was Gisard. Jean-Luc Picard grew up in a pleasant rural setting near Labarre, which he still remembers as the place where his mother, whom he called "Maman," would serve him tea and cookies.

Labarre is a small village near Montreal, France (in the Bourgogne region, consistent with the bottle of 2347 vintage, red, which Robert gives to his brother in "Family") with a 1993 population of 279. The Picard vineyard near Labarre seems to be an established and thriving business, and it is likely Jean-Luc wanted for little materially during his youth.

His sprawling and nostalgic childhood home projected the traditional ambiance of the mid-Twentieth Century French farms. The homestead was kept in the family for hundreds of years, and Picard occasionally returned to visit the vineyards that he played in with his brother during their youth.

Other Picards to whom Jean-Luc may be related include astronomer Jean Picard (7/21/1620 to 10/12/1682), whose determination of the length of a degree of the Earth's surface significantly advanced the accuracy of the measurement of the Earth's overall circumference, and Charles Emile Picard (7/24/1856 to 12/11/1941), a mathematician, and the originator of Picard's Theorem.

Little mention is made of Maurice Picard. Jean-Luc's brother Robert has complained that Jean-Luc was a favorite, and yet something of a disappointment to his father. This must be taken with a grain of salt, but it may contain a germ of truth.

YOUNG LOVE

Young Jean-Luc appears to have had a special relationship with Yvette, as he continued hated piano lessons only to please her. He appears greatly affected by the appearance of her illusory form (as shown in "Where No One Has Gone Before"). They often shared tea, which partially explains the Captain's later predisposition toward that beverage, as well as his morning teas with Beverly Crusher.

Jean-Luc's relationship with Robert is strained. Jean-Luc appears to have been something of a golden child, dedicating himself early in his life to the pursuit of a career in Starfleet, and accepting the standard of near-perfection necessary to achieve that goal. Robert, on the other hand, characterizes himself as hard-working and responsible, qualities he finds lacking in his brother.

Robert believes himself true to Maurice's vision of living the proper life, and resents the attention he lavished on his younger brother. He characterizes his brother as arrogant, an analysis the Captain himself agrees with in "Samaritan Snare."

Robert is not the only person to see these qualities in Picard. Jenice Manheim tells the Captain that he feared an ongoing relationship with her because living in her shadow would have made him "ordinary." (Picard replies: "Am I that transparent?" Jenice finishes: "Only to me.")

Phillipa Luvois says more simply, "You're still a pompous ass."

BROTHER TO BROTHER

Robert currently resides on the Picard estate with his son, Rene, and wife, Marie. The traditionalist resents Jean-Luc's freedom and adventurous lifestyle and constantly reminds him of his dislike of too much technology. This finally erupts into a brawl during one visit, leading to the brothers' reconciliation.

Robert seems almost sadistic, yet strangely protective. As of "Family" it has been nearly 20 years since Jean-Luc last saw his ancestral home. In sharp contrast, Jean-Luc's nephew, Rene, and his sister-in-law, Marie, take an immediate liking to him. Rene has never met him and Marie has made his acquaintance only through correspondence, and the passage of time has mellowed him.

Rene idolizes his uncle and wants to be a starship captain. He has his eyes on the stars just as Jean-Luc always did.

In his youth, Jean-Luc dreamed of reaching the stars. Early in school he wrote an award-winning report on starships, and crafted airships in bottles.

SINGLE TRACK MIND

Jean-Luc was a bright boy. He was the class valedictorian and school president. Young Picard was also a loner with few friends. He had one obsession—to prepare for Starfleet.

Later in life, Picard reflected on that time, attributing his discomfort with

young people to his self-imposed solitude. He has sometimes said he skipped his childhood.

The grown Picard still has difficulty with children ("Encounter at Farpoint," "Disaster," "Suddenly Human"). Interestingly, the Captain manages children remarkably well in "When The Bough Breaks," except for the very young and inhibitionless Alexandria. He also fares well with Jake Kurland in "Coming of Age."

It is notable Picard cautions his nephew Rene against committing himself to Starfleet too early in life. Perhaps he regrets the consequences of his own decision.

It is possible Maurice Picard disappeared early in Jean-Luc's life. There has been little reference to him. Both parents appear to have died long before the events of "Family"—the death of Yvette is confirmed in "Where No One Has Gone Before." This explains Jean-Luc's deep attachment to his mother and his relationship with Robert, with whom he vied for the attentions of their remaining parent.

This accounts for much of Robert's attitude toward the family ancestral home. Marie tells Jean-Luc that Robert has attempted to keep the home looking the same after Jean-Luc noted that it was important to their father.

EARLY MISTAKES

The bond Jean-Luc formed to the fatherless Wesley Crusher is a case of identification. It goes against Picard's natural disdain of children.

When he came of age, a disappointed Jean-Luc failed his first Academy entrance exam. He succeeded on his second try and was admitted with the 2322 class to the Starfleet Academy in San Francisco. Picard was 17.

At the Academy, Picard met Boothby, a groundskeeper and informal guidance counselor. Picard became involved in an Academy scandal similar to that in which Wesley Crusher would later find himself embroiled. The scandal included an error in judgment he ultimately sorted out with Boothby's help (as mentioned in "The First Duty").

During his tenure at the Academy, Picard achieved outstanding academic grades and was labeled a star athlete, most notably as a long-distance runner. He was the first freshman cadet to win the Starfleet Academy marathon.

FULL SPEED AHEAD

Picard graduated from Starfleet in 2237 at age 22 (and was assigned serial number SP-937-215 according to "Chains of Command").at the top of the class of '27 (re: "Samaritan Snare"). It is unknown whether his five terms is standard. It is possible the last year includes a cadet cruise like that portrayed in STAR TREK III—THE WRATH OF KHAN (although no doubt considerably less exciting and taxing).

It is also possible Picard was held back a year, as was Wesley Crusher. This is unconfirmed as Picard and Boothby only made the most oblique references to the "trouble" when they are reunited many years later.

As a cadet Jean-Luc made two lifelong friends, Jack Crusher and Walker Keel. The three were inseparable companions during both their Academy and early service days. In the years to come, Picard would have to deal with their deaths.

Picard's own command decision led to the death of Jack Crusher. His feelings of guilt contributed to his befriending Jack's widow, Beverly, and their young son,

Wesley. There are two different interpretations of Jack Crusher's death.

YOU PICK THE ENDING

In the novel, ENCOUNTER AT FARPOINT, David Gerrold suggests that Crusher was killed by natives on a planetary away mission. He also writes that Picard risked his own life to recover Jack's body.

Yet in the novel, REUNION, Michael Jan Friedman writes that Jack died while cutting loose a damaged warp nacelle. Friedman states that Picard chose to save the ship's Security Chief, Pug Joseph, and left Jack to die. If Picard had returned for Jack, all three would have perished.

Picard returned the body to Beverly Crusher on Terra. "The Bonding" indicated that Picard told young Wesley about the death, while "Violations" and "Encounter At Farpoint" support that he only returned the body.

Picard was indirectly involved with Walker Keel's death. The parasitic conspiracy destroyed Keel's ship, the USS Horatio.

Little of Picard's early career in Starfleet before he assumed command of the U.S.S. Stargazer is known. There are many significant time gaps in what is told of the Captain's life. In THE NEXT GENERATION's sixth season, Picard stated that he had spent 30 years of his career in space (re: "Rascals").

HIS FIRST SHIP

Picard rose through the ranks, serving as Mission Commander and First Officer before being appointed Captain of his own vessel, the Stargazer, registry NCC-2893. It was an older, four-nacelled Constellation class starship used primarily as a deep space charting vessel, much smaller in size and with less crew persons than the Galaxy class USS Enterprise NCC-1701-D.

Picard assumed command of the Stargazer in 2342. In a later conversation with Montgomery Scott, Picard recalls of the Stargazer, "She was overworked. . . underpowered. . . always in danger of flying apart at the seams. But there are times when I would give almost anything to be back on that cramped little bridge."

Upon seeing her again for the first time in twelve years in "The Battle," Picard calls her his "old ship." It may have been the last vessel he commanded before the Enterprise.

Only hints of the Stargazer's missions under Picard have been offered. For instance, she encountered the Cardassians in 2351 (reference "The Wounded"). The ship was in sector 21503 to attempt treaty negotiations when the Cardassians opened fire after Picard lowered her shields. By his own account, the ship barely limped away from the scene of the battle having been stripped of weapons and with her impulse drive damaged.

DAMAGE CONTROL

In 2354 Picard visited Chalna, an anarchic world that is home to the beastly Esoqq in "Allegiance." No details of the mission are available, but but the Esoqq are bipeds who resemble the Kzin in stature and ferocity. Such a world in anarchy could not have presented Picard with an easy mission.

Picard led the Stargazer on an incredible first contact mission that exposed the Federation to hundreds of new cultures. The Stargazer made contact with the Chandra but met its end during first contact with the Ferengi.

DaiMon Bok refers to the encounter as the famous "Battle of Maxia," which

pitted Picard's Stargazer against his Ferengi ship in the Maxia Zeta star system. Until that time, the Ferengi were unknown to the Federation.

During the battle Picard devised a remarkable strategy later dubbed the "Picard Maneuver." It became required reading in Starfleet Academy textbooks. The Captain now refers to it as a "save our skins maneuver." (Interestingly, he noted: "I did what any good helmsman would do." This would seem to indicate that he has not only had helm training, but also that he may have served as a helmsman early in his career. Picard pilots the Enterprise in "Booby Trap.")

After the Stargazer's shields collapsed, when the Ferengi ship returned for another pass, Picard ordered his vessel to increase to maximum warp and close with the other ship. He then gave the order—once the gap was closed—to dump all six photon torpedoes and continue away at maximum speed. The maneuver caused the Stargazer to appear to be in two places at the same time. The Ferengi fired on the wrong ship as the real Stargazer attacked. Unfortunately, although the maneuver destroyed the Ferengi vessel, it failed to save his ship.

Picard's last log entry as Captain of the Stargazer read simply: "We are forced to abandon our starship. May she find her way without us." Picard won the battle, but the dead, burning Stargazer was abandoned. The crew escaped in shuttlecraft, adrift in space for weeks before rescue.

WHO SAID LOVE IS BLIND

Picard was investigated by Starfleet Command concerning the loss of the Stargazer, but was ultimately absolved of all charges. The prosecuting officer was Phillipa Luvois, with whom Picard had his second known romantic attachment. It is difficult to imagine how their relationship might have progressed as his duties kept him in space while hers were decidedly bound to planets and bases.

Differences in ideology, exacerbated by the zeal with which she pursued the case against him, caused their relationship to fall apart. Shortly thereafter, she was either forced to resign her commission (her story) or resigned from weakness (Picard's version).

When Picard sees her again in "The Measure of a Man," she has rejoined the fleet and achieved the rank of Captain. She has been assigned to open a new JAG (Judge Advocate General; the branch of Starfleet responsible for handling internal legal proceedings) office.

Of Picard's Stargazer crew, only Vigo, his Weapons Officer, and Jack Crusher are mentioned by name. Vigo's fate is unknown.

The Stargazer represents three separate areas of possibly contradictory information. First, in "The Battle," her hull is shown largely intact except for minor burns. Her warp drive still functions, and Tasha Yar says that except for six photons, she is "fully armed." She appears viable enough to pose a threat to the flagship of the fleet, the Enterprise. Yet Picard says she was on fire and "finished." Short of anti-matter containment failure, a fire is the worst disaster that can confront a Starfleet vessel. Yet with the Ferengi vessel destroyed, why could Picard not order the surviving crew to safe areas and expose the fire to vacuum, smothering the flames?

CRUSHED

The second Stargazer anomaly concerns Jack Crusher. Crusher leaves a holotape for his infant son, Wesley, recorded when Wesley was 10 weeks old. It is strange that although Jack Crusher lived

another five years (see "True Q") he never visited his son or recorded another holotape.

Perhaps he left additional holotapes with Picard to be given Wesley after certain conditions were met. The holotape in "Family" was, after all, left with Beverly to be delivered to Wesley when he was 18.

The most important Stargazer anomaly is the length of time Picard served aboard her. Various official sources, including the NEXT GENERATION WRITER'S GUIDE, state that Picard served an "incredible 22 years" on the Stargazer. On the other hand, we know he took command in early 2342 and that the ship was lost in late 2354 or early 2355. Thus the Stargazer mission under Picard lasted only about 12 or 13 years, not 22.

There are two possible solutions. Perhaps the Stargazer was slated for a 22 year mission, much as the original Enterprise was slated for a five year mission, but her abandonment prevented the mission's conclusion. A more elegant solution involves Picard on board the Stargazer from 2333 on, beginning as a junior helmsman and moving up through the ranks to Executive Officer.

POOR DECISION

Early drafts of the NEXT GENERATION WRITER'S GUIDE state that Picard was responsible for the regulation prohibiting Commanding Officers from transporting into potentially deadly situations, a regulation he suggested after the tragic loss of one of his captains. The captain who inspired the regulation may have been the original captain of the Stargazer.

The ship would have returned to Earth after the incident for a hearing, after which Picard was installed as Captain. This would explain Picard's reluctance to enter into a long-term relationship with Jenice

Manhelm; he had just witnessed how deadly deep space exploration can be. Picard ignored his own regulation by leading the Away Team on which Jack Crusher died.

At some point Picard became involved in a bar-room brawl (as revealed in "Samaritan Snare") with three Norsicons spoiling for a fight with Starfleet officers. He suffered a near fatal wound when speared through the heart at Farspace Starbase Earhart, in the Bonestell Recreation Facility, an installation apparently filled with galactic riff-raff.

Luckily there was a medical facility nearby which saved him by installing a cardiac implant. Picard once claimed to have been "not much older" than Wesley, sixteen in the second season. He also specifically refers to himself and his comrades as "officers," implying that they had graduated from the Academy. This would place the incident after 2327, making Picard at least 22—six years older than Wesley.

Perhaps, from his current vantage point, Picard feels that a difference of six years is irrelevant, but it occurs at the juncture between adolescence and manhood. It is also possible Picard wants to build Wesley's self-esteem, altering the facts in the process.

During his early years aboard the Enterprise, the implant proved defective. Picard almost died during the replacement operation but was saved by the remarkable medical skills of Dr. Katherine Pulaski.

TIME HEALS ALL

Roughly nine years passed between the loss of the Stargazer and Picard's assumption of command of the Enterprise. It is tempting to interpret this nine year break as a disciplinary action by Starfleet, the result of a black mark on his career.

The problem with this interpretation is that he is given command of the Enterprise, the flagship of the United Federation of Planets. If Picard had a mark against him, or Starfleet had any reason to doubt his abilities, he would not have even been a contender. It is more likely Picard was in command of another vessel between Stargazer and Enterprise.

NCC 1701-D was launched in 2358 and commissioned on October 4th, 2363 (TNG TECHNICAL MANUAL), or Star Date 40759.5 (re: "Data's Day"). Picard took command on Star Date 41124 (re: "The Drumhead"), and his first log is Star Date 41153.7 ("Encounter At Farpoint"). If 1,000 Star Date units equals one year, there was a gap of five months between the commissioning of the Enterprise and the date Picard officially took command.

Picard may have been an adjunct to the team assembling and testing the Enterprise, getting to know his vessel before he took command. He may have met other members of the Galaxy Project team, although both Commander Orfil Quinteros (who led the team that assembled Enterprise; see "11001001"), and Dr. Leah Brahms (who designed the Enterprise's warp engines; see "Booby Trap" and "Galaxy's Child") are strangers to him.

He may have spent this time hand-picking his crew. Picard claims to have hand-picked Riker, and promoted him to Commander for the position of Executive Officer, although as of "Encounter at Farpoint" he apparently has no knowledge of his future First Officer. "We're approaching Farpoint station," he says, "where I'm told a certain Commander Riker will be waiting." Of course, Picard may be being facetious, saying, in effect, "I have never met Commander Riker, but after all I've done for him he'd better be where I have been told he'll be."

DEALING WITH THE PAST

On Stardate 41124, Captain Jean-Luc Picard assumed the Captaincy of the Enterprise, the largest and most advanced Federation ship. TNG's sixth season takes place in 2369. One season of TNG equals about one year of our time. Since the Captain graduated from Starfleet Academy in 2327 ("The First Duty"), twelve years of his career have been planetside or served at a base.

He admits he was undisciplined, loud-mouthed and opinionated. This would seem to justify Robert's opinion of his brother's past behavior.

Beverly Crusher asked for assignment to Enterprise, and her presence is initially discomforting to Picard, who perhaps still feels responsible for the death of her husband. Her attitude toward the Captain is initially cool, but she later warms to him considerably, and their later-seasons relationship appears more friendly than romantic. They share a morning tea similar to that which he shared with his mother.

During Picard's first year aboard the Enterprise, DaiMon Bok returned with the derelict Stargazer, claiming it was found adrift on the far side of the Zendi Sahbu system. Actually the Stargazer was part of his vendetta plans.

The Stargazer was damaged but Picard destroyed the Ferengi vessel. If Picard's original goal for the retrieved Stargazer was carried out, she was delivered to the Zendi 9 star system for refit and repair. She may serving with the fleet.

WILD ADVENTURES

Picard's adventures aboard the Enterprise are many and extraordinary. He has explored a vast array of planets and star-systems, meeting and dealing with many strange alien races.

Most notable is an individual called Q, who fancies himself Picard's chief tormentor. An all-powerful being, Q often takes lessons from Picard instead of being the instructor.

At some point in his early career, according to comments made in "Sarek," Picard attended the wedding of a son of Sarek. This cannot have been Spock as the Captain does not know him when they meet in "Unification." Of course Spock has already proven capable of hiding siblings successfully.

The Stone/Finkas timeline places this event in 2335. It is likely Picard was on planetside duty at this time, perhaps a member of the staff of the Starfleet presence on Vulcan, or a member of the embassy staff Either would explain why a young officer, an Ensign or, perhaps, a Lieutenant, is invited to this very prestigious function. Picard likely witnessed a "humanized" ceremony, not the more private "Koon-ut kal-if-fee" ritual that Kirk and McCoy saw nearly a century earlier.

In Picard's adventures, he deals with time—both past future. In one instance, he traveled six hours into the future to deal with a mobius loop. In another, he and his crew returned to the 1880s in San Francisco to stop an alien invasion. In yet another adventure, Picard and his ship were caught in a false time line and took steps to restore the real one.

QUITE THE REPUTATION

Picard's leadership is admired across the galaxy. On one occasion, he and two other humanoid leaders were abducted by a group of curious aliens in a scientific experiment to study command capabilities.

Jean-Luc Picard often risks his own life for another, whether it be a crew person, his ship, a culture, or an alien being. Captain Picard offered his mind to Sarek as stability for the Vulcan, risking his own sanity. On another occasion, Picard took an arrow in the shoulder on Mintaka to prove that he wasn't a god, after members of Federation accidentally interfered with Mintakan culture.

Picard risked his career to defend Data's android daughter Lol, who was going to be taken away for research by Federation scientists. He defended Data in a similar situation. The Captain even offered his life to stand with his Klingon Security Officer, Worf, as cha'DIch when his late father was accused of treason.

Perhaps Picard's most trying ordeal was when he was abducted by the nearly indestructible Borg, a newly discovered half-human and half-machine race bent on enslaving the galaxy. After kidnapping Picard, the Borg had him physically altered by adding mechanical prosthetics, and incorporating him into their hive.

While enthralled to the Borg, he became the spokesman for the race under the name and personality of Locutus. Picard gathered information leading to the destruction of 39 Federation ships, including four galaxy class starships. Over ten thousand people lost their lives.

Picard was rescued by the Enterprise and restored in time to thwart an invasion of Earth. Peter David described the event as "The Picard Miracle."

Picard revealed to Data how to defeat the Borg hive by putting them to "sleep." Upon recovery and corrective surgery done by Chief Medical Officer Dr. Beverly Crusher, Picard was deemed physically fit but emotionally scarred. A vacation to his family home in France and therapy with ship's counselor Deanna Troi helped him conquer the nightmares from the Borg encounter.

CONTENT

Picard evidently likes his position as Captain and has chosen to remain in space. On Stardate: 41416, Admiral Quinn offered him the position of Commandant of Starfleet Academy. Captain Jean-Luc Picard turned it down.

We also know from "Chains of Command" that the Captain has done a significant amount of research into Theta band transmissions. This also likely occurred as part of his non-space years, and may have included cross-training and temporary transfer to a science branch of Starfleet, much as LaForge was cross-training at the Con bridge position under the auspices of the command division in TNG's first season.

Now in his mid-fifties, Picard is still single and has never married. He also has no known offspring—lucky for him because small children and even teenagers make him uncomfortable. Even though he has proven that he can deal with youngsters in a very paternal, protective fashion, he tends to shy away from such opportunities.

Because of his ambitious nature, always putting career first, Jean-Luc Picard never had time for a long term commitment or relationship. In spite of his career, Picard did manage to squeeze in some romance throughout the years. Over twenty years previous to his stint aboard the Enterprise, a younger Jean-Luc stood up a young woman in a Parisian cafe. Jenice, later known as Jenice Manheim, wife of the noted time-field scientist, was obviously very important to Picard, for when he met up with her again during an Enterprise mission, Picard appeared to almost regret his choice to end the relationship. He obviously had doubted that he made the right decision.

RACING HORMONES

Another romantic encounter took place during one of Captain Picard's vacations from his Enterprise duties. On the planet Risa, Picard met a younger woman named Vash, a rogue explorer on an archeological expedition. Together they shared a few days of adventure and intrigue, and were drawn together by the experience. He told her afterwards that he didn't believe in one-night stands—meaning that the night they spent together meant more to him. In fact, Picard is jealous and protective when she later takes up with the alien, Q.

Vash is the beautiful cross between Indiana Jones and Scarlett O'Hara ("Captain's Holiday," "Qpid"). It is difficult to categorize their relationship, but it is not likely to be exceptionally serious. More reasonably, Vash is a pleasant outlet for the frustrations and anxieties of the duties of Captain who also shares some knowledge of one of Picard's favorite hobby, and who appeals to whatever wildness he suppresses. Vash's very nature makes her unsuitable as a long-term mate for the Captain, and her departure with Q appears to have damaged Picard's ego more than his lifestyle. To his credit the Captain is mature enough to realize the nature of their feelings: "Somehow I think you'd find life aboard a starship," he tells her, "not suitable to your tastes."

Vash is the only sexual relationship Picard forms during the run of NEXT GENERATION as of this writing. Although he certainly formed a strong attachment to Kamala ("The Perfect Mate"), their liaison is best described as genetic level seduction. Like Kirk in "Elaan of Troyius," Picard, or indeed any male, had little choice but to find Kamala "perfect."

Another somewhat romantic encounter for Captain Picard took place almost daily aboard the Enterprise.

Although Picard would be the first to deny it, he often showed more than a friendly interest in his Chief Medical Officer, Dr. Beverly Crusher. Longtime close friends, there is obviously some attraction between the two, but both struggle to keep their relationship on a purely professional level. Perhaps Captain Picard feels a closeness out of responsibility or a protective instinct. He still blames himself for the incident in which he made the command decision that cost her husband his life.

Also on board the Enterprise is another long-time female friend. Guinan, a member of the mysterious, long-lived Listener race, met Picard over fine hundred years ago in 1880's San Francisco when Picard returned to the past. They met again in Picard's real lifetime and have developed a very unique and special trust, although their relationship is purely platonic. Captain Picard has been known to risk the entire Enterprise on her say-so alone. Picard has had many dealings in the past with Guinan, although the nature of these dealings remains a mystery. Guinan says of their relationship that it goes "beyond friendship. . . beyond family," an intriguing clue.

In a more amusing one-sided romantic experience, the Captain is often pursued by the mother of ship's counselor Deanna Troi. Lwaxana Troi, daughter of the Fifth House of Betazed, fails to get Picard's hints and continues to annoy the Captain with her advances.

Captain Picard, however, did get the chance to experience married life, a family, the stability of a home, and even a new culture, when a mysterious probe emitted a nucleonic beam which locked onto him. Picard then experienced an entire lifetime of a man named Kamin on a drought-stricken planet, Kataan.

After futility trying to return to the Enterprise, Picard reluctantly allowed himself to adopt Kamin's life as an iron weaver. His wife, Eline, and Picard had two children, Batai—a son, and Meribor—a daughter. After minutes passed in real time, and decades in Picard's probe-influenced time, the captain is released by the device which was designed to pass along the Kataan history and culture. Surprisingly, Picard appeared quite calm and content, and even enlightened after the adventure.

A MAN OF VALUES

Jean-Luc Picard is a strongly dedicated professional who is firm in his beliefs and opinions, often to the point of being stubborn. He is very duty-oriented and a very staunch defender of Starfleet's Prime Directive of non-interference. In many instances, Picard has fought strongly to uphold his values and the novel beliefs of the Federation. Despite his tremendous leadership potential, and his ability to solve other's problems—even the problems of entire worlds—Picard tends to suppress deep personal issues. In fact, Counselor Troi often presses him to open up and discuss his feelings.

There are many accomplishments which the Federation owes to Captain Picard. He became the first Federation officer to learn the Tamaran metaphor language and is the only Federation officer to successfully negotiate with the Romulans, the Jarada, Quadonians and other races that prove difficult. Picard has been called on as an Ambassador due to his many breakthroughs.

Three times Picard has risked war to prevent war, including standoff with Romulans over advanced technology. He has also negotiated with Cardassians over the corruption of a Starfleet admiral, a renegade Starfleet captain, and his own arrest in a trap designed to lure him for

torture at the hands of the Cardassians who wanted Federation battle plans. He did not break under torture and was restored to command of the Enterprise following the confrontation.

Picard's battle wounds, besides the artificial heart he received after being impaled as a young officer, also include being shot with an arrow by a primitive race who worshipped him as "The Picard" in spite of his protests. He was also seriously injured in a rock slide in an attempt to save Wesley Crusher during their last mission together.

THANKS BUT NO THANKS

Picard was offered an admiralship and the post of Starfleet Academy Commandant at various times. He turned them down but later did return as the commencement speaker at Starfleet Academy. He had a chance there to thank the gardener, Boothby, for teaching him a lesson when he'd made a mistake as a cadet. He found it ironic that he had to teach Wesley Crusher that same message. Cadets joke as they pull their shirts down rapidly, calling it "The Picard Maneuver."

THE MAN AND HIS HOBBIES

Picard enjoys Earl Grey Tea—Hot!, and playing the flute. He is an amateur painter and always finds a way to get out of Beverly's theatrical productions. Picard has served his ship with distinction, even when a Transporter mishap reverted him in body (but not mind) to a twelve year old and still overcame Ferengi invaders to restore control of the ship.

CAPTAIN JEAN-LUC PICARD PROFILE

Strength—60
Intelligence—78
Endurance—68
Dexterity—70
Character—62
Luc—40
Psi Rating—15
Leadership—78
Starship Strategy and Tactics—70
Armed Combat—65
Terran Mystery Novels—60
Small Unite Tactics—56
French History—50
Negotiation and Diplomacy—45
His weaker ratings included:
Human General Medicine—15
Shuttlecraft Technology—20
Starship Helm Operations—27
Federation Law—33
Computer Science—34

Languages:
French—88
Klingonese —30
Galactica (Standard/English)— 60.
Zaranite—44

[Numbers from STAR TREK—THE NEXT GENERATION OFFICERS' GUIDE.]

Picard has been accused of breaking the Prime Directive at least nine times and has repeatedly risked the life of his crew and others to preserve the high ideals which he inspires in them.

Picard is a man of wide and varied interests. His quarters, room 3601 on Deck 9, are a prim example of his diverse tastes. His suite is decorated with artifacts ranging from a sheathed Klingon ceremonial dagger, to an ancient Earth mariner's sextant, to a vintage bottle of family wine on the bookcase given to him by his brother, Robert.

Jean-Luc is a lover of his French heritage and history in general—specifically in archeology. Picard has been studying Iconian culture since his Academy days. He also is a patron of the arts. Jean-Luc often uses classical music to relax, as well as painting. Picard loves reading, preferring a good book over tapes. His literature interests include the works of Earth's William Shakespeare and detective stories such as Sherlock Holmes. His favorite character, another gum-shoe, is Dixon Hill. Picard often chooses to portray the detective in his adventures on the Holodeck.

The Captain also uses the Holodeck extensively for physical activities. He plays racquetball, loves to fence, and enjoys riding. Even though Picard dislikes small animals, he appreciates horses, and often takes his mount through his favorite riding program in the Himalayas Kabul River valley.

Returning to the subject of hobbies, Picard is certainly something of a Renaissance Man. At various times we have seen him interested in horseback riding ("Pen Pals"), fencing ("We'll Always Have Paris," "Time Squared," "I Borg." Barclay fences with a simulacrum of the Captain, along with others, in "Hollow Pursuits," and while it is not strictly fencing, the Captain does engage in some swordplay in "Qpid"), mathematics (attempting to solve Fermat's Theorem in "The Royale"), painting ("A Matter of Perspective;" we have seen no further brush strokes since Data's highly unkind analysis of his work), and music ("A Fistful of Datas").

At least during his academy days he was a runner and a wrestler ("The First Duty"). He has repeatedly been shown to have an interest in literature (he quotes HAMLET in "Hide and Q" from an often-displayed GLOBE ILLUSTRATED SHAKESPEARE, relates to Captain Dathon the story of Gilgamesh in "Darmok," and in "11001001" plans to lose himself "in the pages of an old novel").

Certainly his most serious off-duty pursuit, however, is that of archeology ("Contagion," "Captain's Holiday"). It is interest in archeology that he shares with Vash, and he is knowledgeable enough to be asked to give the keynote address to an interstellar symposium on the subject (see "Qpid").

NO PLACE FOR EMOTIONS

The Captain spends precious little time socializing; most of his hobbies are private, and privately pursued; he is never seen taking part in the Officer's poker game, for instance. Apparently he has always been intensely private and reserved—even somewhat shy. Phillipa Luvois comments, "Overt sentimentality is not one of Captain Picard's failings. Trust me, I would know." When Jenice Manheim confronts him in the conference lounge, she says, "I know you wouldn't come to me." Deanna Troi tells the Captain that it is not easy for him to confront deep personal issues, and that he tends to suppress them.

During his early days in command of 1701-D, Picard displays a great deal of pride in his French heritage, pride that is later noticeably lacking. In "Code of Honor" he tells Data that the French language represented civilization on Earth for centuries, while in "The Last Outpost" he remarks that the French use of the colors "blue, white and red" was in the more proper order than the U.S. arrangement (it is also interesting, and uncharacteristic, that Picard curses, albeit in French, (he says "Merd!") when the full warp pull-away doesn't work in "The Last Outpost").

In "Hide and Q" Picard finds it "ridiculous" that Q is dressed as a Marshal of Napoleonic France. In "11001001" he is delighted to be able to speak French with Minuet. Likely these early remarks were the result of stress at assembling a new crew and taking command of a new vessel, particularly the flagship of the fleet. Lingering subconscious feelings of insecurity may have also contributed to the Captain's belief that the crew should not be witness to his heart replacement in "Samaritan Snare," although equal amount of his natural reserved nature may also be responsible here.

On at least two occasions in a one-to-two year period Starfleet uses Picard in an intelligence role ("Unification," "Chains of Command"). This seems strange as the Federation may be sacrificing one of its premier starship Captains on missions that are likely to be deadly. Indeed, the situation is serious enough in "Chains of Command" that Picard is relieved of command of the Enterprise (Picard is re-assigned to Special Operations, Seltris III), prompting his replacement to comment "Let's be frank, Jean-Luc. This is a one-way mission."

On the other hand, this was also true during the Kirk era; "The Enterprise Incident" and "A Private Little War" were both calculated intelligence missions, and "Errand of Mercy" had strong intelligence elements. Perhaps Starfleet invests a large amount of intelligence training with promising Captains for just such occasions.

It is odd that Picard is re-assigned and replaced, while Beverly Crusher and Lt. Worf, who accompany him on the "one-way" mission, are not. We would expect that a vessel entering a potential combat situation would need a Tactical Officer and a Chief Medical Officer. Perhaps this points to more complicity between Starfleet and the Cardassians, as we have already seen in "The Wounded," and this was all part of the Cardassian plot to capture Picard. Starfleet may have been willing to sacrifice Picard after his encounter with the Borg in "Best of Both Worlds." (Consider how relatively easy it was for the Romulans to brainwash Geordi in "The Mind's Eye;" the Borg could have accomplished with Picard and his crew hoped to do to them in "I, Borg," planting the ultimate mole.) In any event, Picard is still in command of the Enterprise after having undergone not one but two shattering experiences that will doubtless leave permanent marks on his psyche.

A UNIQUE EXPERIENCE

In "Sarek," Picard shares a rare moment for a human, the Vulcan mind meld. Picard melds with Sarek, the father of Spock and Sybok, and is later able to give some amount of comfort to Spock over the loss of his father through the use of a mind tough ("Unification").

Other tidbits of information give clues to Picard's overall character. Being a very private individual, Picard chooses not to discuss politics. He claims he can't dance and attempts it only rarely. Picard also says that he is not a good speller. Picard is not thrilled at taking physicals, and rarely enjoys the "forced fun" of vacations. His serial number is SP-937-215.

Picard has never been married (as revealed in "Samaritan Snare"). Indeed, he tells Wesley that, "Ambitious Starfleet officers must be cautious of long term commitments." Whether this is Starfleet's view or Picard's is left unsaid, but the latter is more likely. On the other hand, his

statement that he has seen his "share of death" (re: "Code of Honor") born out by the known deaths of comrades Jack Crusher, Tasha Yar and Walker Keel may bear out Picard's interpretation.

Captain Jean-Luc Picard's wide and varied interests, combined with his intelligence, experience, physical stamina, and his remarkable leadership talents, all contribute to Picard's near legendary status as the best captain in Starfleet. However, most serving under him, when remembering the Captain, will first recall his trademark phrase when giving an order, "Make it so."

CHAPTER 2

PATRICK STEWART

by Michael L. Ruff, Alex Burleson and David Gardner

Patrick Stewart reveals that he was "compelled" to become an actor, "as a result of an argument." Stewart was born July 13, 1940 to Alfred and Gladys Stewart in Mirfield, Yorkshire England. He was the son of a career soldier and his mother worked as an industrial weaver. Stewart also has two brothers.

When he was twelve years old, Stewart developed an interest in theater. He participated in a drama course and his interest in drama continued. Patrick was brought up in what he describes as "a very poor and very violent household," and spent much of his childhood being afraid. He found that the world of acting provided an escape for him in a number of ways, including having a legitimate excuse to get out of the house at night when he had to go to a rehearsal.

In 1953, young Patrick, an inveterate movie-goer, saw ON THE WATERFRONT and felt transformed by the experience. It was the first time he'd seen a motion picture about a tough and gritty world not all that far removed from his own. It wasn't the usual never-never land of Hollywood that he was used to seeing. He went back and saw the movie four more times, even taking his mother to see it. Stewart remains profoundly impressed by the film to this day, and has managed to meet three of the stars of the film, but has yet to meet Marlon Brando himself.

NEVER LET WORK GET IN THE WAY

At age 15, Stewart left school and landed a job on a local newspaper but his interest in acting distracted him from his job. Although he worked at the newspaper for two years, when his boss made him choose between journalism and acting, journalism lost. That he happened to be an energetic amateur actor wasn't unusual since the English town of Mirfield (population 11,000) supported a dozen dramatic clubs.

"I was always faced with either covering an assignment or attending an important rehearsal or performance," he explains. "I used to get my colleagues to cover for me, but often I would just make up reports. Finally, of course, I was found out. I had a terrific row with the editor who said, 'Either you decide to be a journalist, in which case you give up all of this acting nonsense, or you get off my paper.' I left his office, packed up my typewriter and walk out."

Stewart resented being told how to run his life and decided then and there that acting is what he would do for his career, although he still had to work other jobs to earn a living. For instance, he then worked as a furniture salesman for a year.

"I was better at selling furniture than I was at journalism," Stewart observes good naturedly. As an acting exercise he would become whatever kind of salesman he thought the customer was expecting. He also enrolled in drama school at the Bristol Old Vic to bring his skills up to the level of his enthusiasm. He worked for a year as a furniture salesman in order to save money for tuition.

ON HIS WAY

At the age of seventeen he enrolled in the Bristol Old Vic Theatre. He spent two years at the "Old Vic," both developing his skills and losing the thick accent he'd grown up with. His hair also began thinning at a young age, but while he initially tried to disguise this with hairpieces, he grew more and more uncomfortable with them until he now considers it an affront to be expected to hide, or even have to apologize for, his baldness.

The actor used to see his roles as a way of exploring other personalities and characteristics, but nowadays it has become more of a means of self-expression.

"When I was younger, I used to think in terms of how I could disguise myself in roles. Now I want my work to say something about me, contain more of my experience of the world."

Stewart's professional debut on the stage was in the role of Morgan the pirate in a theatrical adaptation of the classic "Treasure Island." This occurred in August 1959 at the Theatre Royal, Lincoln. After only a month he moved over to the Sheffield Playhouse where he performed until 1961.

When he was twenty-one he joined the touring company of London's Old Vic and traveled to South America and other nations. During this time he worked with the noted actress Vivien Leigh.

In 1962 he returned to the stage company in Sheffield but remained only six weeks. Then from 1962 through 1963 he performed at the Library in Manchester, England. From there he went to Liverpool and acted on the stage at the Liverpool Playhouse into 1964.

Then he returned to the Bristol Old Vic company in 1964, where he'd leaded so much in his late teens several years before. He acted there for two years and met his future wife, choreographer Sheila Falconer. On March 3, 1966 they were married, and the marriage lasted until 1990. They have two children, Daniel Freedom and Sophie Alexander Falconer. His son appeared in the fifth season NEXT GENERATION episode "The Inner Light," playing the son of Picard. Stewart, though, is now divorced.

SERIOUS ACTING

In February 1966, Patrick Stewart made his Royal Shakespeare Company debut at the Aldwych theatre. Stewart has continued performing with the Royal Shakespeare company off and on for some twenty-five years. He's received numerous theatrical awards in his native England, including the Olivier Award for Best Actor for "Merchant of Venice," Best Supporting Actor award for "Anthony and Cleopatra," and for "Who's Afraid of Virginia Woolf" Stewart was given the London Fringe Best Actor Award.

As an associate artist of the Royal Shakespeare Company, Stewart is considered one of the leading talents of the British stage. His impressive list of stage credits include Shylock, Henry IV, Leontes, King John, Titus Andronicus and many others. In 1986, he played the title role in Peter Shaffer's play "Yonadab" at the National Theatre of Great Britain. But the role he covets the most is that of Falstaff. Stewart states, "He is the ultimate creation of Shakespeare—a monstrous, selfish, wicked, devilishly comic, damned, sad man—and I've always been very moved by him,"

Patrick Stewart has become a highly regarded actor in Great Britain from his roles in such BBC productions as I, CLAUDIUS, SMILEY'S PEOPLE and TINKER, TAILOR, SOLDIER, SPY. all of which have aired in America, thus making his work familiar to American audiences as well. His face is also known to American filmgoers from roles in a variety of motion pictures.

In the David Lynch adaptation of DUNE, he played Gurney Halek, one of the more prominent roles in the film. In EXCALIBUR, he played Leondegrance, while in 1985 he was seen in the strange science fiction film LIFEFORCE as the character Dr. Armstrong. Some of Stewart's lesser known films include HENNESSY (1974), THE GATHERING STORM (1974), HEDDA (1975), CODE NAME: EMERALD (1984), LADY JANE (1984), THE DOCTOR AND THE DEVILS (1985) and WILD GEESE II (1985). Stewart also did the voice for an animated feature when he played Major in the 1982 film THE PLAGUE DOGS. He was seen most recently on the big screen in a cameo appearance in the Steve Martin film L.A. STORY.

JUST ONE LOOK

After Supervising Producer Robert Justman saw Stewart on stage at UCLA, the actor was cast as Captain Picard. "A friend of mine, an English professor, was lecturing and I was part of the stage presentation," he recalls. Stewart was doing a literary reading organized by an English professor at UCLA and Justman just happened to be in the audience. Supposedly Justman turned to his wife and stated, "We've found our Captain."

A few days later Stewart was called to audition for STAR TREK—THE NEXT GENERATION. Initially Stewart believed that his would be a more modest role on the series, that of a token Englishman or something like that. When asked recently what attracted him to the part, Stewart stated quite frankly, "Every aspect of it— working in Hollywood, being in a TV series, being in a science fiction series, trying to revive something that had been

successful before—was irresistible. I knew if I said no, I would never know if I might have been able to pull it off."

Since then, he has become a well-known face, although occasionally fans get confused. One woman accosted him at a party and racked her brains until she recognized him. "You fly the Endeavor," she told him triumphantly, when her memory finally clicked, "and you play William Shatner!"

Regarding the fact that Stewart was indeed very much in that role, he once remarked, "As a friend of mine put it when I accepted this job, how do you think it will feel playing an American icon? It did make me a little uneasy. So I'm happy that people seem to have accepted the captain as a non-American. The other thing that has pleased me is that people have written and said you are the crew of the Enterprise, and we believe in that crew. They refer to a vivid contrast between the previous captain and myself, not in a competitive way, but in that they are so different there isn't any sense of overlap."

BALD AND BEAUTIFUL

Patrick Stewart got his biggest surprise when the July 18, 1992 issue of TV GUIDE revealed that in a pole of readers, he was voted the sexiest man on television with 54% of the votes, beating out Burt Reynolds, A Martinez, John Corbett and Luke Perry. He responded to the award by expressing, "Surprise. . . puzzlement. . . and pleasure."

He said that it would have been nice had it happened when he was 19, which is when he lost all his hair and thought no woman would ever look at him again. Stewart had worn a series of wigs over the years and even tested for the part of Capt. Picard by first wearing a hairpiece, but producers decided he looked fine without it. Apparently a lot of female viewers agree with them.

Stewart has grown weary dealing with the inevitable questions concerning his baldness. In an interview in the November 1992 PLAYBOY, Stewart made it clear just how much he resents them. "This is the last time that I will ever discuss my hair—ever, at any time, with any journalist," Stewart told PLAYBOY. "I can never understand it. What if I were to say to you, 'You have an extraordinarily hooked and pointed nose that looks as though somebody got ahold of it and dragged it downward; what are your feelings about that?' You see, I was brought up to believe you do not make personal comments about someone's appearance. It's bad manners. And yet, with baldness it's open season—always.

If I had a huge wart, you wouldn't refer to it. You might keep looking at it, but you wouldn't refer to it. I lost almost all of my hair between the ages of nineteen and twenty. It was absolutely traumatic. I did a number of things to try to prevent it and then, when I saw it was unpreventible, to hide it. But now I have actually been cutting my hair closer and closer. And I think that is the product of beginning to feel now, in my fifties, that it's all right—that I don't have to duck my head."

NEW CHALLENGES

Patrick Stewart moved up to directing in THE NEXT GENERATION in the fifth season and his work includes the excellent episode "Hero Worship," as well as "In Theory" and the sixth season entry "A Fistful Of Datas." But being a series actor has its down side as Stewart is committed to work on THE NEXT GENERATION ten months out of the year.

Twenty-six episodes of the series are filmed a year, and as Stewart explains, "My

day begins at 4:45 a.m. During the spring hiatus of 1991, I discovered this concept of vacation. I went off to Fiji for three weeks and found it not an unpleasant thing. I might go to Alaska this summer," he said in 1992. "I put on two performances of 'A Christmas Carol' there, and my friends promised me an aerial tour so I can pick a place to retire to."

In the early seasons of the show rumors abounded that Stewart was often unhappy with the quality of scripts and that the third season cliffhanger, in which Picard was captured by the Borg, occurred at a point when the actor was threatening to leave the series. These days, though, he is reportedly much happier, particularly with the demands that recent scripts have made of him.

But even in the early days of THE NEXT GENERATION, Stewart recognized that the series was willing to deal with social issues. "I think if we were to adequately explore these elements we wouldn't be making a television series, we'd be doing documentaries. It's present always, though. There's not been an episode where there has not been a central argument dealing with a moral, psychological or social problem. I think Gene Roddenberry takes very seriously, not solemnly, what has to be done with this series and that each story is taking a view of life and has a point of view.

"It's Gene's vision," Stewart added. "We are caught up and embracing that vision and expanding it, but it belongs to Gene. I feel his hand everywhere and I respect it. One of the things that makes this show successful is the sense we have a very distinctive group of individuals working as a cohesive whole."

AN AMBITIOUS GOAL

In the July 18, 1992 issue of TOTAL, a cable TV magazine, Stewart was asked how he feels about the way STAR TREK deals with contemporary issues. "There's something slightly classical about STAR TREK. It's epic, archetypal storytelling. It deals with heroes on a very big scale. It's part morality play. Yet I feel that we have not really addressed certain issues as controversially as we might. I would like to see aspects of the political world of the Federation in the 24th century addressed from a much less utopian point of view. Political life is ambivalent and filled with gray areas. I always felt the show could be more radical politically. My ambition is really a modest one. I just want to change the world."

In 1989 Stewart returned to his first love, the stage, when he began a holiday tradition of performing a stage adaptation of the Charles Dickens' classic "A Christmas Carol." This has been performed most often in New York city during the Christmas season, including on Broadway. The challenge of doing this as a one-man play is that Stewart plays all 35 characters in the story himself. "This role is like running a marathon, and it takes about the same time [just over two hours]," Stewart told PARADE MAGAZINE. "I take a beating and I keep telling people how old I am. Ancient."

Doing this play has been Stewart's way of demonstrating that STAR TREK is just one aspect of his abilities.

The actor is very aware of how closely identified William Shatner and Leonard Nimoy have become with the characters they've played on STAR TREK and one of Stewart's ways dealing with the threat of typecasting is to refuse to use any STAR TREK terminology in the commercial voice-over work he does. "Make it so" and "Engage" are two common terms he has vetoed from commercial scripts he has performed.

Following in the tradition of such STAR TREK actors as Leonard Nimoy and George Takei, Patrick Stewart has read STAR TREK in tape when he read a condensed version of a NEXT GENERATION novel written by Jean Lorrah.

A DIFFERENT MAN

Stewart's style of action has undergone transformations over the years, particularly when he read the play "The Winter's Tale" in 1982. "For the first time I was prepared to directly draw on my own experiences and feelings and instincts in a role. I played Leontes, a monstrously unhappy individual in a play of great beauty and emotional power.

"It's a play about unhappiness, and. . . I understood it," Stewart continues. "I think it was that empathy that enabled me to find something deeper and richer than I found in my work before, and to not be afraid to let my own feelings infect the play. For years, I didn't. For years, I assumed that acting was putting on something from the outside rather than discovering it within you. I want to see an actor show me himself as much as I want to see the role in the play. I'm not interested in fancy tricks or technical fireworks—that's very quickly boring. I want to be touched by something else."

Stewart revealed that when his contract is up in 1993, "I'm planning to do classical theatre, 'Lear' and 'Macbeth.' I'm the right age now to play the heavies."

His forthcoming non-STAR TREK work includes roles in ANNIE AND THE CASTLE OF TERROR and two crime dramas in which he'll portray the "heavy."

THE COMMANDER

JOHNATHAN FRAKES - Headshot at the building dedication, Paramount.

Photo: © 1993 Ortega/Ron Galella Ltd.

Number One, second in command to Captain Picard, and the dynamic young leader of many an Away Team. His history in its own way is as unique and exciting as Jean-Luc's.

CHAPTER 3

COMMANDER WILLIAM T. RIKER

by Kay Doty

The entire Riker family rejoiced when a son was born to career diplomat Kyle Riker and his wife Elizabeth after seven years of marriage. Kyle, the youngest of three siblings, was the first to give their parents the grandchild they longed for.

They named the healthy eight pound child William, and the letter T, to allow him the privilege of selecting his own middle name when he became older.

Kyle's duties required that he be off planet, frequently for months at a time. Not wishing to place her son in the keeping of professional caretakers, Elizabeth opted to place her own successful career as a botanist on hold to be a full time mother during Will's formative years.

The arrangement worked well, but Kyle's long absences from their home in Valdez, Alaska were often a strain on both wife and son, resulting in deep emotional ties between Elizabeth and Will. On the rare occasions when he was home, Kyle would take Will out into the cold Alaska air and point out the various stars where he had served. When duty called and it was time to depart, Kyle left maps of the stars and their planets with their names printed in bold letters. He marked the places where he would next visit with a large red X.

Will developed a burning desire to read so that he could study his father's maps without help—and he did so. By the time he was three years of age he knew the names of all the stars on the map as well as many of those stars' planets.

WRITTEN WORDS

From the very beginning Will was an excellent student, but he was also a normal boy who loved to play games with his friends. The games he enjoyed the most were those whose theme was space travel. Strangest of all was his interest in books. Even though the public entertainment that was piped into all homes was easier, Will enjoyed the printed word.

The boy didn't know exactly what a diplomat did, but he knew what starships were, and almost before he knew much else, he knew he would some day captain one. When Elizabeth explained that it took many years of study, plus serving in subordinate positions before one could become a ship's captain, Will responded, "That's all right, Mama. I will study and I will serve in those positions, but some day I will be captain of the greatest ship of them all."

Elizabeth had no doubt that he would, but she would not live to see his dream fulfilled. One day when Will was eight years old he came racing home from school to show his mother his latest project, only to find her lying in a pool of blood on the bathroom floor—

dead at the age of forty of a brain aneurysm.

Will's first thought was that his mother had fallen and banged her head, causing a nose bleed or some other minor injury. When he couldn't rouse her, he ran the two blocks to the home of his Uncle Girard. When the med team arrived Will watched, still and frozen, while they attempted to revive her.

"Where are they taking her? When will they bring her back?" Will screamed as Elizabeth's body was carried from her home.

Girard, along with his wife, Rainey, tried to comfort the boy, who couldn't believe that his mother was gone forever.

"She loves me! I know she wouldn't leave me," he cried over and over until his voice was reduced to a hoarse whisper. At last too weak to resist, he was led from his own home to that of his aunt and uncle.

EMOTIONALLY TROUBLED

They tried to comfort him while they waited for Kyle. Will ate, at least a little. He bathed, changed his clothes and went to bed and got up when told to do so, but Will did not cry again. Most of the time he remained in the bedroom they had provided for him, staring out a window which overlooked the front walk—watching for the one person who would never use the walk again. Toward the end of the third day, he overheard Girard tell Rainey that Kyle's shuttle would arrive within the hour. Will put on his favorite jacket, a gift from Elizabeth, and slipped unseen out the back door. He couldn't explain, even to himself, why he didn't want to see his father.

Kyle arrived in Valdez three days after he received the news of Elizabeth's death—to find his son missing. Grief

stricken almost beyond the ability to comprehend what had happened, he simply did not believe that Will's absence was serious. He refused to leave the room containing his wife's body, allowing his brother Girard to worry about Will.

Kyle was devastated. From the time he was a high school senior and Elizabeth was a freshman, they had known that some day they would marry—not a contract, but a real marriage. Neither ever had eyes for anyone else. Like Will, Kyle could not perceive that she was gone forever. Even as he stood looking at her as she lay peacefully in her coffin, he fully expected her to sit up and laugh at the elaborate hoax she had perpetrated, just to see the look on his face.

Girard instigated the search for Will, calling all of his friends, his teachers and the neighbors, but it was Rainey who found him. She remembered that Elizabeth had frequently taken Will to a small lake a short distance from town. On a hunch she went to the lake and found him lying face down in a shallow cave sobbing into the jacket. Settling down on the rock floor of the cavern, she gently pulled the grieving boy into her lap. She didn't try to hush him, knowing the tears were the beginning of the healing process.

As Rainey's tears mingled with those of her nephew, the sobs that had racked his body slowly began to subside. She never quite remembered just how long they sat together sharing their grief—five minutes, ten, a half hour? It didn't matter for his first comment was forever etched in her mind.

"It's all my fault she went away."

"William, how could your mother's death possibly be your fault?" Rainey blurted out, shocked.

"Because I was bad; so bad that she couldn't stand to be with me any more—why else would she leave?"

"Oh, my poor darling, you weren't bad! You never were. Her death wasn't, it couldn't have been your fault. Something just went wrong in her body—something so terrible that the medics and doctors couldn't fix. Your mother loved you! She wouldn't have left you of her own free will." Rainey pulled him closer, gently rocking him as she recited many of the good times he and his mother had shared.

"She was so proud of you. She would be very sad if she knew you were blaming yourself for something that no one could have imagined happening."

Will appeared to be comforted. He had certainly needed the tears to cleanse his aching heart. As they returned, arm-in-arm to the house, Rainey hoped she had purged the guilt from his mind. She would never know how many years would pass before a dedicated ship's counselor would help him to purge that guilt himself.

A GROWING DISTANCE

The memorial service was subdued and attended only by the family, a few friends, and a representative of the diplomatic corps. Kyle Riker stood ramrod stiff, dry-eyed and staring at nothing. When his son reached for his hand, he did not respond—perhaps in his grief he didn't notice—but it was the first in a long series of events that would drive a wedge between Will Riker and his father.

Kyle requested, and was granted, a post that would allow him to remain at the Federation Embassy in San Francisco. He made a determined effort to make a home for his son, but his own grief went too deep for him to realize how badly the boy needed him. Will spent more and more time with Rainey and Girard, and avoided his father.

The situation was too explosive to remain as it was—and it didn't. With a child's wisdom, Will knew that Kyle missed Elizabeth as much as he did, and suggested

they take a walk together. Hand-in-hand they left the house with Will leading the way—Kyle's mind was on other things.

They arrived at the lake where Rainey had found Will before Kyle realized where they were going. When he saw the water lapping against the shore, he was furious. This had been their special place, where on a certain tree, long ago, he had carved his and Elizabeth's initials inside of a lop-sided heart. A short distance away stood the bench where they had shared their first tentative kiss. He abruptly yanked his hand free of the boy's, his face contorted in grief.

"How dare you bring me here!" he raged at the boy. "How unfeeling can you be. This was our special place, hers and mine. We never shared it with anyone." Kyle was too caught up in his own grief and pain to realize Will had no way of knowing that.

"It was our place, too. We came here lots of times," the frightened boy yelled back, not understanding what he had done to evoke such anger in his father.

"Well she had no right to share it with anyone—not even you!" Kyle's voice was sullen, the shock dissipated some of his anger, but not enough to explain the reason for his rage—to apologize. And then it was too late.

"It's your fault she's dead! Your fault! Your fault!" Will charged at his father and began pounding with with his fists. "If you'd been home she wouldn't have got sick! You didn't take care of her. Your fault, fault." He had to pass his own stored up guilt on to someone, and that someone was his father. Will began to cry, still feebly striking Kyle's body, as the storm within him began to weaken.

"Will . . . Son . . . " Kyle began, catching the boy's hands in each of his own, but he got no further. Will jerked away and ran blindly away from the lake. Neither would ever visit that site again.

BLATANT ATTEMPTS

From that point on the relationship between Will and Kyle was strained. Will now believed that his father also blamed him for his mother's death and didn't love him any more. He tried desperately to make amends, to show that he hadn't meant to do anything wrong—to make his father understand that he loved and needed him.

Will brought home school projects to share. He did extra chores around the house, brought school mates home to meet my "Dad," and chattering incessantly about Elizabeth until Kyle's nerves would snap and he'd order the boy to be still. Hurt and angry, Will would go to his room, slam the door and try not to cry. Kyle was becoming a polished diplomat but hadn't the slightest idea how to repair the growing chasm between himself and his son—a son that he deeply loved.

A year after Elizabeth's death, an explosive situation developed between two new member worlds of the Federation, and Kyle was ordered to join the negotiating team to mediate a peace treaty. Facing the prospect of being gone for many months, Kyle closed the house and sent Will to live with Rainey and Girard, who were happy to have him.

Will was frightened. First his mother had left him, and now his father. Fearful that Kyle too would go away and never return, Will begged him not to leave and couldn't understand Kyle's explanation. Furious, the boy climbed into his tree house and refused to come down until after the man's departure. Kyle called out "Good-bye" and promised to see him soon, but received no reply.

The first couple of weeks with Girard and Rainey were a trial for everyone. They could understand the boy's grief and fears, but it couldn't go on. His grades had taken a nose dive, his clothes looked as he had slept in them—and perhaps he had. He got into fights at school and his reply to any question put to him was a sullen shrug of his shoulders.

MAN TO MAN

One evening as Will lay face down on the living room floor, his head cradled in his arms, Girard motioned for Rainey to leave them alone.

Quietly he suggested it was time for a man-to-man talk. Not by sign or word did Will indicate he'd heard, but Girard began to talk. He said that life wasn't always fair, but everyone, including children, had to make the best of a bad situation. He said that Kyle had a job to do, and like it or not, he had to go where the job required—but he would be back.

"You say you want to be a starship captain," Girard continued, "but you'll never make it behaving as you are. That would hurt not only you, but all of us who love you. But most of all you would be tarnishing your mother's memory. She never had any doubts that you could do anything you set your mind to do. She didn't die on purpose and would never have left you of her own free will, but where ever her spirit may be, it is your job to live your life in a manner that would make her proud."

Will did not respond or give any indication that he had heard, however the following morning when he came down to breakfast, his clothes were nest, his hair combed, and he replied quietly to Rainey's "Good morning." If anyone noticed the redness around his eyes, and they did, no one commented.

For the first time in over a year, Will began to relax and live a normal life for a little boy. His grades improved, he picked no more fights, and was courteous to his teachers. More than ever he was determined that one day he would captain a great ship.

A pattern was established. Kyle would return from a mission and Will would return home—then another assignment and Kyle would be gone, for weeks, months, and once nearly two years, and Will would return to Rainey and Girard.

During the periods when Kyle was home, Will was required to do many of the household tasks. The growing boy resented being ordered to do these chores even though he enjoyed some of them, such as gardening and cooking—a fact he would never admit to his father.

A MUSICAL ESCAPE

Despite the antagonism between himself and his father, or perhaps because of it, Will spent more time pursuing his love of music. It became an escape, a way to avoid Kyle, but he didn't allow anything to interfere with his school work. He knew that only people with top grades were admitted to Starfleet Academy, therefore studying was always his uppermost priority.

An event occurred just prior to Will's eleventh birthday that would also play a role in shaping his life. Friends of his aunt and uncle were killed in a shuttlecraft accident. In their will they had named Rainey and Girard guardians of their thirteen year old daughter, Musetta-Elinor.

The girl was bewildered and in pain, not only by the loss of her parents but the change in lifestyle—from traveling the galaxy with her celebrity musician parents, to living a quiet life in the small Alaskan town.

Because he was near her age, Musetta-Elinor confided in Will, pouring out her grief. He understood and listened. Slowly her pain began to recede and the two "orphans," as they dubbed themselves, became inseparable. She laughed at his steadfast devotion to jazz and taught him

the classics, explaining that the first half of her name was taken from an ancient Earth opera. His private name for her was M-E and she called him Billy, a name he detested coming from anyone else.

He told her about the stars, his desire to attend Starfleet Academy and some day command a ship, and when she expressed an interest in the Academy, they decided to attend together and she would be his first officer. They would sail off among the stars forever.

TOO MUCH PAIN

Will was happier than at any time since Elizabeth's death. For his fourteenth birthday, Rainey and Musetta-Elinor threw a party for him. Kyle had promised to be there, but at the last minute sent his regrets and a gift—a box of star maps. Will kept them, not because they were from his dad, but because they were valuable study aids.

His M-E knew how hurt and angry he was and gave him a beautifully crafted model of the first Enterprise. In his excitement he didn't notice that she was not her usual vibrant self. She became moody and snappish and complained of being tired. When she fainted and couldn't be revived, she was rushed to a hospital. After a battery of tests she was diagnosed as having ZYZX Chromosome Syndrome, a fatal disease that affects one in ten million teenage girls. The origin was unknown, and there was no known cure.

Will sat at the bedside of the comatose girl, talking, begging her to hear him, to speak, to fool the medical profession and get well. He reminded her of all their wonderful plans, to no avail. Rainey, the doctors, and well meaning friends urged him to go home, telling him that the dying girl could not hear him, but he refused to leave her.

Hours later, with her hand still in his, he was dozing, his head resting on the bed when he felt a slight movement. He jerked awake to see that her eyes were open, a slight smile on her lips.

"Billy," she whispered and squeezed his hand with what must have been her last ounce of strength, "you must sail the stars for both of us; I'll be there somewhere." Then she closed her eyes for the last time—the smile still on her lips.

UNFAIR VOW

Will was inconsolable. Once again someone he loved deeply had left him. He made a solemn vow never to allow himself to care that much about anyone again. It would be over twenty years before he would meet a beautiful dark haired woman who would shatter that vow.

Will graduated with honors a year and a half later, and just prior to his sixteenth birthday placed first in the Starfleet Academy entrance exams. He was on his own.

Although the incident was never mentioned, Will had heard and remembered those earnest words spoken by his uncle, so many years earlier. He had established a study criterion that assured him a spot among the leaders in all his classes.

Years later Will would admit that he was pretty grim during his academy days (and even after he went on to Command school), although at the time he considered himself dedicated. His instructors were happy to have so able and willing a student in their classes. He wasn't the only one who was always prepared, but he was one of the few who took dozens of extra courses in all phases of starship operation.

This isn't to say he didn't loosen up and have a good time on occasion. He made friends easily and was always a favorite when they could drag him to a party or other outings. Will was attracted to the female cadets in his classes, and they to him. He dated frequently, but no one girl for any length of time, particularly if he found himself beginning to have strong emotional feelings for a special girl. Saying that his goals made it necessary that he remain unencumbered, he always broke off the relationship. Perhaps his subconscious mind still remembered the vow he made at the memorial services for his beloved "foster sister" Musetta-Elinor.

COMPLETELY DEDICATED

Rather tan spend all for his spare time pursuing romantic adventures, Will and his best friend, Telller Colon, developed a personal workout regimentation that was not only the envy of the other cadets for keeping fit, but enabled them to consistently place among the leaders in both the required, and optional, physical and mental endurance classes.

Riker spent long hours in Starfleet archives purusing the logs of three centuries of both Federation and alien ships. He wanted to learn routine duties as well as the dangerous missions, away-team resourcefulness, and how to protect oneself and other away-team members. It didn't take him long to realize that being in top physical condition could mean the difference between life and death. Cadet William T. Riker had not a doubt in his mind that some day he would be commanding such teams, and their lives would depend on him making the right decision.

When friends urged him to forget ancient history and relax a bit, Will insisted that the histories of the men and women who had pioneered the exploration of the stars was relaxing. But he enjoyed the company of his classmates, and was enthusiastic when they invited him to join their frequent musical jam sessions. He tried playing a variety of instruments, but eventually settled on his first love—the trombone. During his junior year he formed a five-piece jazz ensemble, conducting as well as playing.

Rainey and Girard proudly watched as Will graduated from the Academy at the top of his class. He hid his disappointment, saying it wasn't important, when Kyle, now an ambassador for the Federation, sent his regrets. Delicate negotiations in a distant part of the galaxy demanded his participation, making a return to Earth in time for the ceremony an impossibility. Kyle did, however, make his son a solemn promise that he would be in attendance when Will graduated from Command School.

Kyle had every intention of keeping that promise, and in truth had sent a message on his way home when the starship on which he traveling was attacked and their warp drive knocked out. The engineers worked hard but the best they could do was warp two. He arrived four days after the ceremony only to learn that Will, along with his friend Conlon, had shipped out on the Potemkin. There would be no further communication between father and son for over fifteen years.

THE REAL THING

The thrill of actually being assigned to his first post and on his way into deep space after all the years of study was intoxicating. And a starship at that, even if it was one of the smaller ones. To be sure he'd been out in space on training missions, and had even been a trainee commander, but there was always a classroom to which he must return. In contrast this—this was REAL!

It was also true that he was only an ensign and had to take orders from almost everyone on the ship, but that was the way it worked. He knew all about the chain-of-command, and he intended to climb that chain as quickly and fairly as possible.

Ensign Riker worked hard, accepted any and all assignments and volunteered for others, while always aware of the danger of being over eager. He won promotion to Lieutenant, Junior Grade, in record time. Two years later, after an especially nasty mission when the away-team commander was captured and seriously injured by hostile forces, Riker took command. He not only masterminded the return to the ship of the remaining team members, but persuaded the opposing forces to release his commander.

For this action he received a commendation and promotion to full lieutenant.

After five years on the Potemkin he transferred to the Yorktown as second officer. Now a Lt. Commander, Riker knew he was on his way to achieve a goal. Friendly and cheerful, he was well liked and crew members followed his orders willingly.

However it was on the Yorktown that he met the one person who nearly shattered his vow to remain unencumbered.

IRRESISTIBLE

Lieutenant Deanna Troi was the most beautiful woman he had ever met. The waves of dark hair floating down her back, coupled with her snapping black eyes and ivory skin, was a combination that was hard to resist— and Will didn't. He knew she was half human and half Betazoid, and was concerned that she could read his mind. She assured him that she could only read emotions, not actual thoughts, but even during their most intimate moments, she knew he could not completely commit himself to her.

Although he denied it to himself at first, it didn't take Will long to realize he was in love with his charming shipmate, and she with him. They spent much of their off duty hours together. She taught him to communicate silently with her in the manner of her people—a gift she had been unable to share with any other human. He would come to know her as he had never known another person. Because of their strong emotional attachment, a link was formed that in the years to come, particularly during moments of great peril, their minds would reach out to each other, even across great expanses of space.

It was because of Deanna that Will committed the one cowardly act of his life. After three years on the Yorktown, and while Deanna was on leave, he transferred to the Hood as the ship's first officer. He knew it would be impossible to tell her good-bye in person—he would stay or take her with him—so he ran. He believed, at the time, that a permanent emotional attachment would hinder his career plans, but he could never get her out of his mind and his heart.

Now a commander, Riker served his ship and captain well. He not only earned the respect and loyalty of the crew, but their friendship as well.

NEW BEGINNINGS/ OLD FRIENDS

Another three years and again he was ready to move on. Learning that the new captain of the newly commissioned Enterprise, 1701-D, the flagship of the fleet, was in need of a first officer, Will applied for and was granted the transfer, with his new captain's approval.

His new commander, Captain Jean-Luc Picard, was unlike any other he had ever served under. It did not, however, take the two long to earn the other's respect and friendship. The two worked well together and assembled a crew that under their leadership established the new Enterprise as the pride of Starfleet.

But it was on the Enterprise that Riker learned a valuable lesson—one can't ever completely run away from something—or someone. On his second day aboard he unexpectedly came face to face with the Ship's Counselor, Deanna Troi, his old love.

In the beginning there were many uncomfortable moments between them before they moved forward into a mutual satisfying, and very special friendship.

Two years after joining the Enterprise, Riker was offered his lifelong goal—his own command. The captain of the explorer ship Area was retiring and it was Riker's for the taking. The ship was small and assigned to a little explored part of the galaxy. Not only would he be in command, but the probability of many exciting adventures appealed to his explorer nature.

The excitement of the possibility of command was dulled when he met the civilian ambassador who came aboard to brief him—Kyle Riker, his estranged father!

ACCEPTANCE

Kyle came aboard hoping to make amends, but Will was unforgiving. After several heated arguments, they met for a match of anbo-jyutsu, a violent game they had played during Will's boyhood. Many emotions surfaced during the game. They stopped blaming each other for past events and/or transgressions, real or imaginary, confessed their love for each other, and parted friends.

his career would be better served by remaining on the Enterprise.

He was later offered the Melbourne, but before he could make a decision the ship was destroyed by the Borg.

Riker was appointed Captain of the Enterprise during the war with the Borg after Captain Picard was kidnapped by the Borg and thought lost forever. With the help of his very able crew, Riker not only defeated the enemy, but rescued Picard. He willingly returned to his position as first officer.

Picard has also turned down two promotions, to Admiral and a position at Command Headquarters, to remain on the Enterprise. Will he one day accept and leave Riker to command the Enterprise? Only time will tell.

CHAPTER 4

JONATHAN FRAKES

by Kay Doty

Unlike many aspiring performers, Jonathan Frakes received solid family support when he announced his decision to follow a professional acting career.

Born in Bellfont, Pennsylvania and reared in nearby Bethlehem, Frakes is the son of a college professor who taught English and literature. Professor Frakes was also a sometimes drama critic and movie devotee, therefore when the younger man announced his intentions to pursue an acting career, he had the full support of his family.

Jonathan first became enthralled with acting while participating in junior high and high school plays. Upon graduation he enrolled at Pennsylvania State University as a psychology major, but his love for theater persisted. He soon became involved in a small off-campus professional group. He was not only impressed with his fellow thespian's enthusiasm for their work, but that they were paid for doing something they loved.

Soon thereafter he switched his major from psychology to theater arts. Upon graduation from Penn State with a Bachelor of Fine Arts and Theater Arts, he spent two summers at Harvard studying drama where he performed in the prestigious Loeb Drama Center.

After college, Frakes moved to New York where he became a member of "The Impossible Ragtime Theater."

AN AMERICAN HERO

A distant cousin to his acting career was the work he did for Marvel Comics during his early New York days. Wearing a Captain America costume, along with Charlie Davis who portrayed Spiderman, the pair carried garbage can lid shields and appeared at shopping malls, super markets and grand openings of various businesses. They rode on the hoods of cars to attract attention, answering questions from non-believing children. Frakes later commented that they humiliated themselves for $50.

The high point of his Captain America career came when he was invited to the White House by Rosalynn Carter to be one of the entertainers at a lawn party for daughter Amy Carter and friends.

During the lean years, Frakes also donned a red suit and pillow to play Santa Claus in various New York department stores. The Impossible Ragtime Theater performed serious drama authored by well known playwrites, both living and dead. One of these was "The Hairy Ape" by Eugene O'Neill, in which Brian Dennehy was one of his cast mates. Next he was chosen as a replacement for a cast member of the Broadway musical "Shenandoah."

"I gave myself a five year limit," he reveals. "If I wasn't making a living at acting in five years, I would find something else to do. After a year and a half of being the worst waiter in New York and screwing up my back as a furniture mover I got a role in 'Shenandoah' on Broadway and then landed a part in THE DOCTORS." Then his career was off and running.

From Broadway stage, Frakes moved on to the world of soap opera with a year-long role on the now defunct THE DOCTORS. His character was a dark, sinister child-beater who was later "killed" in a nightclub fire, effectively ending his stint on the soap.

WIFE AND WORK

Frakes' next move was to the west coast where he played guest roles on various television shows and mini-series. One of these was BARE ESSENCE where he met Genie Francis, the former GENERAL HOSPITAL star. They met again three years later during the filming of the critically acclaimed mini-series, NORTH AND SOUTH, and were married in May 1988. Frakes also appeared in the sequel to that mini-series, NORTH AND SOUTH: BOOK II.

Some of the other shows in which he appeared before becoming second-in-command of the Enterprise include DREAM WEST, PAPER DOLLS, FALCON CREST, THE WALTONS and the television movie version of THE NUTCRACKER. He was frequently cast as a villain and is enjoying playing a nice guy for a change.

When the casting call went out for STAR TREK—THE NEXT GENERATION, Frakes answered. He was impressive enough to be called back seven times over a six week period before being cast as Commander Riker. He admits to some expert coaching from Gene Roddenberry.

"I knew this was a real part, a big one," says Jonathan Frakes regarding the six weeks of auditions he went through for the role, "and I had to get it."

A NOTE OF THANKS

The actor credits Gene Roddenberry with giving him the needed insight into the character that eventually became his.

"Gene is so very non-Hollywood and really quite paternal. One of the things he said to me was, 'You have a Machiavellan glint in your eye. Life is a bowl of cherries.' I think Gene feels that way, which is why he writes the way he does. He's very positive and Commander Riker will reflect that," states Frakes.

"I think Roddenberry's gotta be pretty pumped up he turned the networks down," Frakes said when it was clear that the series had become a hit. "He had such a. shitty time with them the first time. We did a scene where I call Q a son of a bitch and no one even suggested I do it another way. I think they're going to try and push the limits a little. It's interesting because Roddenberry stories always have little morality plays and so to carry it into the actual production of the show makes the line very thin as to what's appropriate and what's not. I'm curious to see how it's drawn. To have it put in the creator's hands is a very powerful position and I love it. I think he likes it and I hope handles it appropriately. One wonders if it's appropriate to call someone an S.O.B. at 6 o'clock on Sunday night."

Fraker felt that one of the highlights of the first season was the episode "11001001." "A fabulous show. Those were the kind of chances we took first season that when they worked, they worked great. It was a very chancy show and I loved it. Those character, the Binars, why haven't they returned? That was a very well conceived idea. They should have them as a regular on the ship to fix the engines or whatever the hell they do.

"I think we took greater chances then than we do now," Fraker adds. "The shows may be better, the level of it, but 'Skin of Evil' was absurd. We had Patrick sitting and talking into a black oil slick— but what was wrong with that? I suffered physically like a fool with Mikey—sure, I'll get in that black f***ing metamucil shit. That was absurd. That was a time first season when they took chances. Some of it misses, but some were great. Like 'Naked

Now,' the episode which we've never done anything quite like where everyone got drunk and horny. That was risky. All the early stuff with Brent as Sherlock Holmes. Bowman's work, the first Klingon show— those were all great."

FAST BECOMING A FAVORITE

During the long hiatus between the first two seasons, due to the writer's strike, Frakes grew a beard, mainly because he dislikes shaving. Roddenberry liked it, and the beard is now a part of Riker's character.

Frakes congenial nature make him a favorite on the convention circuit, but one con he isn't likely to forget occurred at Boston on September 21/22, 1991. After fans were seated in the ballroom of a large hotel, many arriving hours early to assure themselves of a good seat, the management announced that there had been a mistake and the room had been reserved for a wedding reception.

The grumbling fans were moved to the bar, a location not near big enough to hold all of them. From there they were herded into the hotel parking lot where they waited for an impromptu stage to be erected. Frakes was more than a little surprised when he realized he would actually be performing in a parking lot. He took the bizarre situation in stride, joked about not being invited to the wedding, and royally entertained his delighted fans. His appearance the following day was in its regularly scheduled location, inside the hotel.

As much as he enjoys the role of Commander Riker, Frakes also had an eye on the director's chair. After consulting with producer Rick Berman, Frakes spent over 300 hours studying the various aspects of directing. His turn at the helm

came in the third season with "The Offspring" in which Data creates a daughter. The episode was well received by fans and producers alike. He has since directed four more episodes—"Reunion," "The Drumhead," "Ethics," and "Cause And Effect."

The actor sees Riker, the executive officer and second in command of the Enterprise as, "strong, centered, honorable and somewhat driven. His job is to provide Captain Picard with the most efficiently run ship and the best prepared crew he can. Because of this he seems to maintain a more military bearing than the other characters in behavior, despite the fact that salutes and other military protocol no longer exist in the 24th Century."

Frakes' only criticism of the show is that after portraying Riker as a man anxious to gain a command of his own, he turns down three opportunities. But his enthusiasm for the show remains high, and he says he'll remain as long as they want him. He would also like to see THE NEXT GENERATION cast do a movie after it concludes its television run.

TRULY GRATEFUL

Commander Riker has, on occasion, played the trombone, not surprising since the actor has a passion for the instrument. He prefers jazz and says he would like to some day play in a Dixieland band. While that goal may be down the road a ways, he does sit in at a local night club when his 10-12 hour days permit.

When Brent Spiner made the album "Ol' Yellow Eyes Is Back," his backup singers were the Sunspots. The name was a logical choice since the singers were his fellow space travelers—Frakes, LeVar Burton, Patrick Stewart and Michael Dorn. This is just one example of how well the cast get along with each other. Said Frakes,

"I don't know how they cast this so well. We go out to dinner after fourteen hour days. They hired actors who like to act instead of hiring movie stars or models. For virtually all of us, this is the biggest job of our career and we're so happy about that. It's an ensemble and I think it's a good ensemble."

In February 1992, Frakes joined Enterprise shipmates Patrick Stewart, Gates McFadden, Colm Meaney and Brent Spiner in two sold out performances of "Every Good Boy Deserves Favour" at the Don Wash Auditorium in Garden Grove, California. The very successful stage production was a benefit for the Orange County Symphony and Amnesty International.

"I really have been very lucky. There's a cliché in this business that says, the easy part of being an actor is doing the job. The hardest part is getting the job. I think we realize how fortunate we are to be working in an industry where 98% of actors are unemployed at any given moment."

LIEUTENANT COMMANDER

BRENT SPINER - At the Creation Convention Q&A with the cast at the Bonaventure Hotel. Photo: © 1993 Ortega/Ron Galella Ltd.

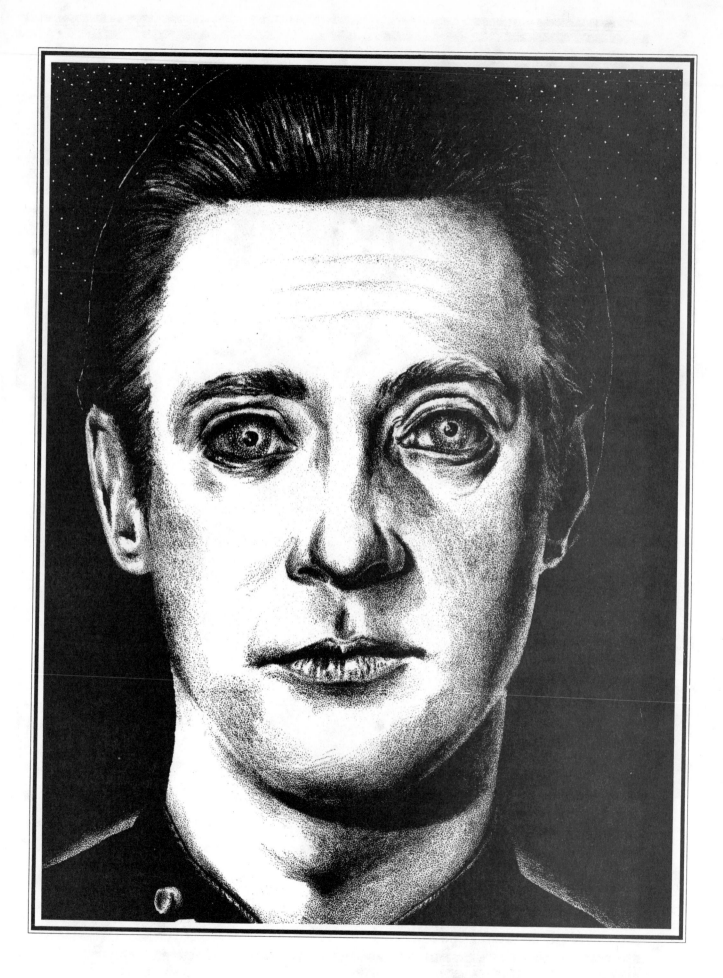

"The Enterprise has its share of aliens aboard, but it has only one android, and his name is Data.."

CHAPTER 5

LIEUTENANT COMMANDER DATA

By Lt. (j.g.) Diane K. McCarty

Dr. Noonian Soong had been Earth's foremost robotic scientist until he made wild promises about his positronic brain design (inspired by 20th century Earth author, Isaac Asimov). Soong worked diligently, but his attempts were met with failure after failure, earning him the nickname "Often Wrong Soong."

With his reputation ruined, Soong went to the scientific colony of Omicron Theta under an assumed name. There, he and his assistants continued to work on designing their android, and finally perfected it. They named their creation "Lore." Lore had superior strength and superhuman mental faculties coupled with the personality of a human and ability to understand human idiosyncrasies, such as humor. He even had emotions and was a fully functional humanoid male (i.e. anatomically correct). In fact, he was perhaps the first "perfect" being ever created.

However, soon Lore proved to be too perfect. He was superior to humans, and he knew it. With the help of his self-teaching neural nets, Lore found a way to circumvent the three laws of robotics* which Soon had programmed into him. He developed an arrogance which caused some consternation among the colonists. They petitioned Dr. Soong to disassemble Lore and create a less perfect android. Soong endeavored to do so when he created his next android, which he left unnamed.

He left out of this android an "emotions chip" so that the android would have more trouble interfacing with Humans. The hardware for this new android was virtually identical to Lore's. Soon afterwards, an energy/life absorbing crystalline entity threatened the colony, and they built a protective shielding to hide themselves.

Faced with the threat of the entity, Dr. Soong stored the factual information gathered by all the colonists into his new android, including their personal logs and journals. He used digitized memory transfer technology developed by his colleague and one-time teacher, Dr. Ira Graves. The transfer did not include the colonists' day-to-day memories, however, but the accumulation of factual information. This later inspired the android to name himself "Data."

IN THE NICK OF TIME

Shortly after the completion of Data's construction and programming, the crystalline entity overcame Omicron Theta. Guided by Lore, it destroyed all life on the planet, even soil bacteria. Utilizing Lore's "off" switch, Soong managed to disable him at the last minute. He disassembled the android and preserved him in a cryogenic storage unit. Soong escaped the attack of the crystalline entity in a cargo shuttle.

He transplanted himself and his personal possessions, including most of the equipment in his laboratory, to an uninhabited planet. Before he left, he placed Data on a stone slab outside the protective shielding with a signaling device which would lead any humans to him and "awaken" the android upon their approach.

Some time later, the Starfleet vessel U.S.S. Tripoli was dispatched to Omicron Theta. Led by the signaling device, an Away Team discovered Data. The android awakened, not knowing who he was or how he'd gotten there. The crew of the Tripoli brought their discovery to the proper Federation authorities, and found themselves embroiled in a fierce controversy.

Some argued that the android was dangerous and should be dismantled. The captain of the Tripoli, Caroline Victoria Gorden, argued before the Federation Special Investigation Committee on Stardate 29904 that Data was not an inhuman monster, but more like an innocent child—one clearly programmed with the three laws of robotics. Furthermore, she adopted Data as her "child." The Committee, guided by intensive investigation by a number of noted cyberneticists, agreed with the captain's arguments, declaring Data to be no threat to humanity. In addition, they found that Data was, in fact, a living being.

ROUGH GOING

Scientists at the time were fascinated with Data and, with Ms. Gorden's permission, examined him at length. His physiology became the subject of several biomechanic texts. Captain Gorden aided Data in his somewhat difficult integration into society, eventually sponsoring his entrance in Starfleet Academy a mere four years after his activation.

Starfleet administrators consulted a large number of robotic experts and all of them agreed that Data should be accepted into the service—except for one. A young prodigy, Dr. Bruce Maddox, argued, "I believe the Soong android should be protected. We should keep it at the Daystrom Institute. Can you imagine how much we can learn once we take it apart and examine its design? We could eventually learn to replicate it. Dr. Soong's genius need not be lost. But it will if you let it expose itself to unknown dangers."

Nevertheless, Maddox's arguments fell on deaf ears and Data entered the Academy after passing every entrance test, not the least of which was the much dreaded "psyche test." He worked his way diligently through his Academy training, excelling scholastically, but he could never quite fit in with his classmates socially.

Data's inability to understand the concept of humor distanced him from his fellow cadets and he was naturally the butt of many practical jokes. Social gatherings were particularly awkward for Data, especially a Sadie Hawkins dance. He graduated with the class of '78 with honors in Probability Mechanics and Exobiology.

Data was then assigned to a number of ships, most notably the USS Trieste, NCC 37124, a Yosemite class starship. He was promoted through the ranks until he achieved the rank of Lieutenant Commander. Assigned aboard Starfleet's new flagship, the USS Enterprise, NCC 1701-D, Data was given the duties of Second Officer and Chief of Ops. He was now 26 years "old."

Data distinguished himself aboard the Enterprise, and what follows is but a few of the highlights of his notable service aboard the ship. [The author would like to express her gratitude to Mr. Data for providing substantial logs of the missions, including word-for-word transcriptions of his excerpts from personal logs.]

SAVING THE DAY

The maiden voyage of the Enterprise began on Stardate 41153, under the command of Captain Jean-Luc Picard. The ship encountered a super-powerful being which called himself "Q." The being arrogantly commanded the humans to return to Earth and, when they refused, he put them on trial for being a "grievously savage race." Data functioned in the role of court reporter at the trial, being called upon to recite part of the proceedings verbatim. He also assisted in solving the mystery of Farpoint station, a test which proved to Q that he was a little too hasty in judging the humans.

On Stardate 41209, the Enterprise rendezvoused with the USS Tsiolkovsky, a science vessel investigating the collapse of a red giant into a white dwarf. The ship's crew died due to actions resulting from an intoxicating infection that had spread throughout the ship. The infection soon infiltrated the Enterprise. Data was not immune to its effect, acquiring it from Security Chief, Lt. Natasha Yar, who lured Data into her bed.

After the experience, Data was to tell Captain Picard, "We are more alike, than unlike. . . I have pores; humans have pores. I have fingerprints; humans have fingerprints. My chemical nutrients are like your blood. If you prick me, do I not. . . leak?" After the collapse of the star, the ship was unable to move, due to an assistant chief engineer who, infected with the disease, pulled out the engine control chips. Data was enlisted to put them back, and his actions helped save the ship. A cure was found for the disease and things returned to normal. But, much to Data's confusion, a regretful Yar dismissed their previous intimacy, telling him "it never happened."

When Q made a second appearance, he gave William Riker an offer he couldn't refuse: the awesome power of the Q. Riker used the power to give each of his friends their fondest wish. He was about to make Data a human, when the android stopped him. "I never wanted to compound one illusion with another," Data explained. "It might be real to Q, perhaps even to you, sir, but it would never be so to me. Was it not one of the captain's favorite authors who wrote, 'This above all: To thine own self be true.'?"

THE EVIL TWIN

On Stardate 41590, the Enterprise stopped briefly at Omicron Theta. There they discovered Lore's body in Dr. Soong's old laboratory, took it aboard the ship, and reassembled it. Lore was clearly more human than Data, the only glitch in his system being an apparent eye tick. Lore appeared to wish to please humans more than Data. However, he tricked Data into drinking laced champagne which disabled him. Lore then assumed Data's identity and lured the crystalline entity to the ship. Wesley Crusher discovered the deception and his mother reactivated Data. He stopped Lore from giving the crystalline entity the life of the people on the Enterprise and Wesley beamed the errant android into space.

On Stardate 41602, the Enterprise encountered a "skin of evil" which called itself Armus. The creature tried to force the Away Team to entertain it, but they defied it at every turn. It struck down Lt. Yar, killing her. Later, at Tasha's funeral, a prerecorded message of Tasha's farewell speech was played. "My friend, Data," she said, "you see things with the wonder of a child, and that makes you more human than any of us." Afterwards, Data said to Captain Picard, "My thoughts are not for Tasha, but for myself. I keep thinking how empty it will be without her presence."

On Stardate 42437, the Enterprise flew to Gravesworld, home of Dr. Ira Graves. Unbeknownst to the Enterprise crew, the dying scientist transferred his consciousness into Data's body before his own body died. Liberated by his new body, Dr. Graves made advances to his assistant, Kareen Brianon, with whom he had fallen in love. But her rejection of him invoked violence, however unintentional. Captain Picard convinced him to vacate the body to avoid any further "accidents." Data's personality regained control of his body and Graves stored his vast knowledge in the ship's computer—but the human equation was gone.

Data's existence was met with a more serious threat when Dr. Bruce Maddox appeared on the scene, meeting with the Enterprise at Starbase 173. Again, Dr. Maddox wished to disassemble Data in order to understand the android's workings and replicate it. Data rejected his proposal on the grounds that "His basic research lacks the specifics to support an experiment of this magnitude." Not to be deterred, Maddox produced a document ordering Data to transfer off the Enterprise and to allow the experiment.

Maddox assured Data that his knowledge and memories would be downloaded. But Data replied that they would be "Reduced to mere sterile facts of the events. The flavor of the moment could be lost. . . There is an ineffable quality to memory that I do not believe can survive the shutdown of my core." In other words, Data believed it would mean his death. He had no escape but to resign from Starfleet. Maddox challenged this and Captain Phillipa Louvois, the local Judge Advocate General, in accordance with an old, outdated law, declared Data property of Starfleet—he couldn't resign.

Furious, Captain Picard objected to the ruling. Captain Louvois then presided over a hear in which—due to a lack of staff—Picard argued in Data's favor and Commander Riker was compelled to argue in favor of Maddox. Riker proved that Data was a machine, one capable of being turned off. Captain Picard called Maddox as a hostile witness, forcing him to expound the three basic tenets of sentience: intelligence, self-awareness, and consciousness.

Maddox admitted that the android had intelligence, and his behavior before and during the hearing made it clear that he was concerned for his own survival—thereby making him self-aware. Picard then drove Maddox into a state of confusion such that the man didn't even know if Data was alive or not. Picard turned to Captain Louvois with this: "Starfleet was founded to seek out new life. Well, there it sits, your honor." He pointed at Data. "Will you condemn him and all who come after him to servitude and slavery?" Louvois ruled that Data was not the property of Starfleet and that he had the right to choose. Naturally, Data chose not to participate in Maddox's experiment. He did, however, tell Maddox that he found some of the man's work "intriguing."

PROVING HIS WORTH

At the beginning of his third year aboard the Enterprise, Data was assigned to convince the human colonists living on Tau Cygna V to leave their planet. A race called the Sheliak had claimed the planet for their own according to the Treaty of Armens. Unfortunately, most of the colonists, under the leadership of Gosheven, wished not to leave their home. With the help of Ard'rian McKenzie, and a strategically pointed phaser blast, Data was successful in his mission.

On Stardate 43539, Q again graced the ship with his presence. This time, he had been stripped of his powers (but not his arrogance) by his fellow Q. Data was assigned to watch over Q and keep him out of trouble.

Data also introduced Q to some of the basic concepts of being human. He taught Q more by action than by word, saving his life from an attack by the vengeful Calamarain.

In so doing, Data nearly sacrificed his own life for the man and Q could not understand why—he wouldn't have returned the favor. "There are creatures in the universe who would consider you the ultimate achievement, android. . . " Q told him in Sickbay. "But if it means anything to you, you're a better human than I." Q took off in a shuttlecraft, nearly sacrificing himself to save the ship, when the other Q gave him his powers back. Q paid his debt to Data by giving him a gift: he made him laugh—which was to Data, "a wonderful feeling."

On Stardate 43779, the Enterprise transported mission specialist Tam Elbrun, a Betazoid with highly developed telepathic talents, to the Beta Stromgren system. There he established first contact with an entity known as "Tin Man." It was a living ship, alone and roaming through space without a crew. Elbrun found Data's presence preferable to that of the rest of the crew because he could not read the android's thoughts and was therefore not distracted by them.

Elbrun established contact with Tin Man while the ship was still many light years away. When he and Data beamed over to Tin Man, Elbrun established a symbiotic relationship with the being. As Data was later to tell Counselor Deanna Troi, "Through joining, they have been healed. Grief has been transmuted to joy, loneliness to belonging. . . When Tin Man returned me to the Enterprise, I realized this is where I belong."

A FIERY FATE

On Stardate 43872, Data was assigned to transport shipments of the volatile substance hytritrium. The chemical was obtained from the trader Kivas Fajo. As he was about to transport the last shipment, Data was captured by Fajo's assistant, Varria. They sent the unmanned shuttlecraft back en route to the Enterprise with a bomb aboard, and it exploded in space. The Enterprise crew were horrified to see what they believed to be Data's destruction.

Geordi found it hard to believe that Data was really dead. He tried to piece together some clues that seemed to indicate that his android friend was still alive, despite discouragement from Captain Picard. Accepting Data's death with characteristic stoicism, Picard opened a book of Shakespeare, which he had once given Data, and read, "He was a man, taken for all-in-all. I shall not look upon his like again."

A very much alive Data awoke to find himself the latest acquisition of Fajo's prized collection of rarities. He defied Fajo's every command until the trader threatened Varria's life. Now his ally, Varria helped Data to escape, but was caught in the attempt and cruelly killed by Fajo. When Fajo threatened to kill more people to insure Data's cooperation, the android picked up Varria's weapon and aimed it at him. "I cannot allow this to continue," Data told him. He pulled the trigger. Just at that moment the Enterprise crew, having solved the mystery of Data's "death," beamed him aboard just before he could kill Fajo with the weapon. Fajo's collection of "toys"—illegally obtained— was confiscated and he was turned over to the proper authorities.

PATERNAL INSTINCTS

On Stardate 44085, Data, in response to a homing signal transmitted by Dr. Noonian Soong, hijacked the

Enterprise to Soong's new home. He beamed down to the planet and met his father for the first time. Data asked Soong, "Why did you create me?" The scientist responded by asking Data why people are interested in old things. Data replied, "Perhaps for humans, old things represent a tie to the past. . . They seem to need a sense of continuity. . . To give their lives meaning, a sense of purpose. . . I suppose it is a factor in the human desire to procreate." Soong responded, "So you believe that having children gives humans a sense of immortality?" This, the old man assured him, was the answer to Data's question.

When Lore showed up, it was apparent that Soong's homing signal had affected him as well. Lore was surprised that Soong was still alive. He explained that he would still have been floating out in space had it not been for a Pakled ship which picked him up. Soong revealed his reason for bringing Data there: he had developed a special "emotions chip" for the android that would make him perfectly human, like Lore.

Lore became envious of his brother and deactivated Data while Soong took a nap, locking him in a closet. Soong then implanted the chip into Lore, believing him to be Data. After the operation, Lore began to exhibit highly unusual behavior and let Soong know who he really was. Soong warned him that the chip wasn't designed for his circuits, but Lore lashed out with violence at him and escaped via Transporter back to the Pakled ship. The Enterprise Away Team beamed down and reactivated Data. In a moment alone with Soong, Data had a chance to say goodbye to his father.

On Stardate 44215, the Enterprise went to Earth colony Turkana IV, home planet of the late Tasha Yar, in response to a distress call from a Federation freighter. The crewmen aboard the freighter had escaped to the planet in a pod. The Enterprise discovered that a Turkanan faction called the Alliance was holding the crewman of the freighter hostage. The Away Team made contact with the Alliance's enemies, the Coalition. Its leader introduced them to one of his people, Ishara Yar, Tasha's sister.

She acted as a liaison to help the Enterprise rescue the hostages. Data told her that he and Tasha had been close friends. He explained his ability to feel friendship for someone thus: "As I experience certain sensory input patterns, my mental pathways become accustomed to them. The input is eventually anticipated and even missed when absent."

Ishara and Data began to develop their own friendship and she even spoke of possibly leaving her home for Starfleet as her sister had done before. But, unbeknownst to Data, she was really using his trust in her to serve her own purposes. Ishara and an Away Team beamed into the heart of Alliance territory, where she led them to the hostages. As the team was freeing them, Ishara sought out the Alliance's fusion generator and triggered it for self-destruct.

Data stopped her from this, realizing that she had used him all along. Nevertheless, Ishara insisted that the time they had spent together had been the closest thing to friendship that she'd ever had. Upon Captain Picard's order, Ishara was turned over to Coalition authorities. Afterwards, Data found it very hard not to think about her.

UNAFFECTED

On Stardate 44502, the Enterprise encountered the Paxans, a highly xenophobic race of beings. They created an illusionary wormhole and knocked out the crew—all except Data, who was not affected. He told them that they had been unconscious for 30 seconds and that the wormhole had thrown them a day's travel from the planet. When the crew began to find clues which indicated that a full day had actually passed, they began to suspect that Data was lying. Picard ordered the ship back to Paxan space. A Paxan took control of Counselor Troi and insisted that the ship must be destroyed in order to protect the Paxans' anonymity.

Data revealed that this had happened once before and that everyone's memory had been erased regarding the occurrence—except his own. Picard had ordered Data never to reveal the existence of the Paxans—hence his motivation for concealing the truth from his fellow shipmates. With the Paxan's permission, they recreated what they had done before, but this time, they made sure not to leave any clues.

Near the end of the fourth year of the mission, Captain Picard acted as arbiter at the installation ceremony of Gowron as Leader of the Klingon High Council. He ruled that Gowron should be the leader and not the son of Duras. Because Duras' family had strong support, the Klingon Empire was plunged into a civil war in which the two factions fought it out.

On Stardate 45020, Captain Picard told Starfleet Command about his suspicions that the Duras faction was in league with the Romulans. He was put in charge of a fleet of ships which were deployed at the Romulan border in order to detect any possible Romulan contact with the Klingons. Data was put in command of one of these ships, the USS Sutherland. His first officer, Lt. Command Christopher Hobson, objected to serving under an android and requested a transfer. Data denied it. The Romulan emitted a tachyon field, designed to distort the fleet's sensors so that they might slip through. Picard

ordered the fleet to drop back and rendezvous at Gamma Eridan.

Data disobeyed the order and stayed behind, using the sensors to detect tachyon signatures around the cloaked Romulan ships. Hobson defied Data every step of the way, reminding him of Picard's order. But, once he'd found the Romulan ships, Data ordered Hobson to fire on them. He did so, reluctantly. The Romulans, realizing they'd been discovered, returned to their own space, leaving Duras' family unprotected. Gowron's faction won the war.

CAVE MEN

On Stardate 45122, Data and an Away Team were present at the Melona IV colony when it was attacked by the crystalline entity. They survived by taking refuge in a cave. Dr. Kyla Marr, a scientist who had made the study of the entity her life's work, was called in to investigate. An obsessed hatred of the entity was deeply ingrained in her because her son had been among those killed by the entity on Omicron Theta. She blamed Lore for the deaths and transferred some of the distrust of the android to his brother, Data.

Nevertheless, she soon learned to trust Data by working closely with him. They discovered a gamma radiation trail which led to the entity. They also found a way to begin communication with it. But, against orders, Dr. Marr destroyed it by having the Enterprise emit a continuous gravitron beam. Data did not approve of the action for it violated their mission to seek out new life.

On Stardate 45236, Picard was shown a recording of Vulcan Ambassador Spock in the company of Romulan Senator Pardek on the planet Romulus. It appeared possible that Spock had defected and Picard was ordered to find Spock and bring him back to Vulcan, if possible. Data and Picard voyaged to Romulus in a cloaked Klingon ship. Although they were disguised as Romulans, their presence was detected by Pardek's men, who led them to Spock.

The ambassador explained that his intent was to discuss possible reunification between the Vulcan and Romulan peoples with Senator Pardek and others sympathetic to the cause—including, seemingly, the Proconsul himself. Unfortunately it turned out that Pardek and the Proconsul were in league to deceive Spock. Captured by the half-Romulan Sela (daughter of Tasha Yar and her Romulan captor), Data and Spock used computer-generated holograms to effect their escape. Data incapacitated Sela with a Vulcan nerve pinch.

A MATTER OF PROTECTION

On Stardate 46315, Data met Dr. Farrell, a roboticist who had created the Exocomps—enhanced servo-mechanisms capable of performing new tasks by replicating new circuitry and new tools. When an Exocomp refused to obey orders which would have put it in danger, Data believed it had a sense of self-preservation. Furthermore, he suspected that the Exocomps were alive.

Data performed extensive tests on one of the machines, but finally it was the Exocomps' own actions which proved their sentience. Data explained his actions to his captain. "When my own status as a living being was in question, you fought to protect my rights. The Exocomps had no such advocate. If I had not acted on their behalf, they would have been destroyed. I could not allow that to happen." Picard

replied, "It was the most human decision you've ever made."

A diligent worked whose energy never fatigued, Data nevertheless occupied his off time with a number of interesting diversions. He constantly strived to understand the human equation, which unceasingly eluded him. Unsuccessful at telling jokes, he turned his attention to artistic pursuits, taking up painting and music as hobbies. The android distinguished himself in the latter, learning to play a number of instruments, including the oboe, guitar and violin.

He played solo violin in a string quartet performed for Vulcan Ambassador Sarek. Data was also fascinated by ancient Earth fiction, most notably Sherlock Holmes and Dixon Hill. Data's emulation of Holmes and his methods of deduction helped him solve many a mystery which lay ahead. He made good use of the holodeck to act out the characters of Holmes and "Carlos," a persona he created when play-acting in the Dixon Hill universe.

Coached by Captain Picard, Data enhanced his understanding of humans by acting as characters in certain plays, including the title role in Shakespeare's "Henry V" and Scrooge in a dramatization of Dickens' "A Christmas Carol." Data was a student of method acting. "Since I have no emotional awareness to create a performance, I am attempting to use performance to create emotional awareness," he told his captain. "I believe if I can learn to duplicate the fear of Ebenezer Scrooge. I will be one step closer to truly understanding humanity."

His attention turned to games and he hosted a poker party. This became a regular gathering for several of the bridge crew, including Commander Riker, whose bluffs Data often fell for. When Dr. Beverly Crusher taught Data how to dance, it inspired him to program a 17-step dancing tutorial—with some rather interesting partners—on the holodeck.

GAINING ACCEPTANCE

Data's integration and interaction with humans reached new heights during his mission on the Enterprise. He developed a close friendship with Geordi LaForge, who joined him on the holodeck as Dr. Watson to Data's Holmes. There's no question that all of the bridge crew developed a liking for the mechanical man and all considered him a friend. Captain Picard became somewhat of a father figure for Data, serving as a role model on his quest for humanity.

Data even had a girlfriend, Jenna D'Sora, for a brief period of time. He created a special romance program for her (which he deleted when the relationship broke up). He was once a "father of the bride," giving Keiko Ishikawa away in her marriage to Miles O'Brien. Data's participation in the ceremony triggered a certain curiosity about marriage in general, and he spoke of his interest to Counselor Troi. "Although I am an android, I have not excluded the possibility that I, too, may some day marry. I believe I have much to offer a potential mate." Data's friendships were not limited to intelligent species. He adopted a cat, named him Spot, and even composed a poem for the pet.

Most intriguing of all was Data's relationship with his "daughter," Lal, an android he created. Captain Picard expressed some concern over the ramifications of this creation of new life. But as Data explained to him, "I have observed that in most species, there is a primal instinct to perpetuate themselves. Until now, I have been the last of my kind. If I were to be lost or destroyed, I would be lost forever. But if I am successful with the

creation of Lal, my continuance is assured. I understand the risks, sir, and I am prepared to accept the responsibility." As Lal's father, Data taught her the basics in life: how to eat and drink, and how to recognize and appreciate art and beauty, among others.

LIVING ON

Unfortunately, his attempts to instruct Lal on integrating socially with humans met with less success. She was entered in the ship's school where she could not mix well with the other children—they were afraid of her and she didn't understand their humor. Lal did show promise, however. She developed the ability to speak with contractions—a skill Data had never attained. When Admiral Haftel of the Daystrom Annex on Galor IV heard of Lal's creation, he tried to bring her to the institute for further study.

Data objected to the Admiral's orders. "I have brought a new life into this world and it is my duty, not Starfleet's, to guide her through these difficult steps to maturity," Data explained to his captain. "No one can relieve me from that obligation and I cannot ignore it." After the admiral spoke to Lal about her possible relocation, she became afraid, not wishing to go.

The emotion caused her to malfunction and a cascade failure began. Her neural pathways collapsed too quickly for Data to repolarize in time. She was dying. Just before her death, Lal told Data, "I love you, Father." Not all was lost, however. Data incorporated Lal's programs into his own memory. In essence, she lives on inside of him.

I would like to close with this quote from Data's personal log: "There are still many human emotions I do not fully comprehend—anger, hatred, revenge. But I am not mystified by the desire to be loved or the need for friendship. These are things I do understand. If being human is not simply a matter of being born flesh and blood; if it is instead a way of thinking, acting and feeling, then I am hopeful that one day I will discover my own humanity. Until then, I will continued learning, changing, growing and trying to become more than what I am."

THE THREE LAWS OF ROBOTICS
as developed by Dr. Isaac Asimov:

(1) A robot may not injure a human being or, through inaction, allow a human being to come to harm.

(2) A robot must obey the orders given it by human beings except where such orders would conflict with the First Law.

(3) A robot must protect its own existence as long as such protection does not conflict with the First or Second Law.

CHAPTER 6

BRENT SPINER

by Diane K. McCarty

Brent Spiner was born in Houston, Texas on February 2, 1949. He has one brother, Ron, who is two years older. At a young age he lost his father. His mother, Sylvia Mintz, later remarried. Between the ages of five and thirteen, Spiner was entertained every evening by the musical talents of Frank Sinatra, Judy Garland, Nat "King" Cole, Rosemary Clooney, Louis Prima, Keely Smith, and many other artists whose recordings were included in his stepfather's elaborate collection.

This musical feast later inspired him to release his own recording of pop standards on an album entitled (somewhat tongue-in-cheek) "Ol' Yellow Eyes is Back" (1991). Between the ages of eleven and fifteen he became an avid movie fan, watching three movies each day (excluding THE AFRICAN QUEEN, which he plans to save for his death bed). His favorite movie is "The Searchers" starring John Wayne.

The young Spiner attended Bellaire High School, where his mentor was his drama coach, Cecil Pickett, whom Brent would later describe as "one of those remarkable people who set you on a course for the rest of your life."1 That is most certainly true in Brent Spiner's case and that of his classmates: Dennis and Randy Quaid, Cindy Pickett, and Robert Wuhl, to mention a few. Pickett left Bellaire in 1968 to teach at Houston Baptist University and the University of Houston and Spiner went with him to further his studies. He also attended Trinity College and the Strassbourg Institute of New York, among others.

Spiner's early professional life was full of its ups and downs, and the young actor earned his dues, auditioning for play after play, some of which were more than a little shy of Tony Award-winning caliber. Most notably short of glory was "The Portable Pioneer and Prairie Show," a play he had the dubious honor of performing in while living in Chicago. Spiner was later to dub it, "one of the worst plays ever written."

GETTING BETTER

Fortunately there are some brighter spots on Spiner's resume. After he arrived in New York, Spiner supported himself by driving a cab for six months. He landed his first role at a "cattle call" (an open audition). After that, he managed to support himself as a full time actor. He appeared in "Polly" (a sequel to "A Beggar's Opera") and "The Crazy Locomotive" (both off-Broadway). He portrayed Kil in "The Family" (1975).

Drama critic Clive Barnes praised Spiner as "admirably nutty as the knife-fingering brother." A year later he played a variety of roles in "Marco Polo": an interpreter, a mime, a dragon, a giant, a henchman and a Chinese girl. In "A History of the American Film" (1978), a musical montage of parodies on various film genres, he appeared as Hank. Spiner incorporated into his role clever impersonations of Henry Fonda, Jimmy Stewart, Gregory Peck, and Anthony Perkins (a la Norman Bates).

That same year he appeared in the award-winning mini-series THE DAIN CURSE on CBS, playing Tom Fink, a special effects wizard. In 1980 he landed a role in a bizarre tribute to the 1970's entitled "Leave It to Beaver is Dead." Spiner's character, Luke, is a tabloid photographer who shoots faked scenes of gory events. Later that year, he appeared in the two-man show, "Emigres" as the nameless character "AA," an intellectual political refugee. Critic Mel Gussow rated him thus: "Spiner enlivens his performance with a whiplash nervous energy and physical limberness. Scarcely missing a beat, he swerves from good fellowship to wounding abrasiveness. He makes his character unpredictable."

With his career well in swing, Spiner spent the first half of 1980 as the Older Son in "Table Settings." This well-reviewed comedy centered around a Russian-Jewish grandmother, her two sons, and their families. He appeared in the film STARDUST MEMORIES with Woody Allen. In his cameo scene, Spiner played a "Fan in Lobby" snapping Polaroids of his idol. This autobiographical portrait of Allen's life presaged Spiner's own experience as a celebrity.

He wrapped up the year in Chekov's "The Seagull," in the role of Konstantin Treplev, a suicidal playwright. Spiner was later to refer to this play as, "the one that finally pushed me over into the serious actor category." Unfortunately he suffered a back injury on opening night which forced him out of the production. He spent six months recovering from the injury and it haunts him to this day—he threw his back out during the filming of the NEXT GENERATION episode "The Silicon Avatar."

STAYING BUSY

Work was hard to come by after that, but he landed his first leading role (and, to date, his last) in a low budget flick entitled RENT CONTROL.

Spiner returned to the stage in "No End of Blame" as the 2nd Male Nurse (1981-

82) and "Marvelous Gray" (1982). The title of the play was the name of an infant who died under mysterious circumstances. Spiner's role, the Electrician, was part of a TV crew which covered the story. The play focused on how the media affects public opinion. Sometime later, Spiner again performed in a Chekov play, "The Cherry Orchard" as Pyotr Trofimov, a philosopher.

In the latter part of 1983, Spiner played the part of John Polly in "The Philanthropist," a role which was rather short-lived (no pun intended). John is a playwright reading his play's ending to a critic and a philologist—an ending in which the lead character kills himself in front of two other men. The critic finds the ending unbelievable, so John acts it out for him. Unfortunately, he ends up blowing his head off.

Spiner then headed for the Broadway stage and played two roles in the award-winning musical "Sunday in the Park with George." The play brought to life people in 19th century painter Georges Seurat's famous creation, "Sunday Afternoon of La Grande Jatte." The play consists of two acts. Act One takes place in the 19th century, with the central character, George (brilliantly brought to life by Mandy Patinkin) working with persistence on his new style of painting despite harsh criticisms by his peers.

In this act, Spiner played Franz, a coachman with a fondness for the bottle, and an intense dislike of his employer's bratty daughter. In Act Two, which fast forwards to the twentieth century, he played Dennis, a former NASA technician who helps Seurat's great-grandson (also named George) build his hi-tech laser artworks. The play was received to enthusiastic reviews.

A PART OF HISTORY

Not everything was coming up roses for Spiner in 1984. Cast in the part of

Aramis, Spiner suffered through the grossly mismanaged musical "The Three Musketeers" (1984), which he described as "maybe the worst Broadway show of all time. . . I think it lost more money than any show in the history of Broadway, which is some distinction." The show was produced by the Ringling Bros., Barnum and Bailey Circus. The initial producer had died of a heart attack and his son decided to carry on the show in his memory. Plagued with technical difficulties, "The Three Musketeers" bombed and only lasted one week.

Spiner moved to Los Angeles and, naturally, his career took a turn toward television. He dropped in on TALES FROM THE DARKSIDE as the whiskey swilling Reverend Peabody in "A Case of the Stubborns" (1984), a minister who had the difficult task of convincing a dead man to lay down in his grave as was proper.

In the miniseries ROBERT KENNEDY AND HIS TIMES (1985), he played Allard Lowenstein, a political supporter of the Senator during his presidential campaign. As an attorney named Hinnerman, he defended a judge (played by Andy Griffith) in CRIME OF INNOCENCE (1985). The judge had sentenced many juvenile offenders to serve time in adult prisons. One of these, the lead character, had been raped by a guard while in jail, and her parents sued the judge.

He did a guest spot on PAPER CHASE as Charles, a law professor's assistant. He appeared as hotel manager Clinton Waddle in the failed pilot of SYLVAN IN PARADISE which featured Jim Nabors as the bell captain. He wrapped up 1985 by returning to Broadway to play The Duke in "Big River," a musical based on THE ADVENTURES OF HUCKLEBERRY FINN. And he played the lead role of Seymour in "Little Shop of Horrors" on stage in L.A..

BAD CHARACTERS

In 1986, Spiner played Jim Stevens in the TV movie MANHUNT FOR CLAUDE DALLAS, a man who watches the title character murder two forest rangers who tried to stop him from hunting illegally. He also dropped in on several shows for guest appearances. On HILL STREET BLUES he brought to life Larry Stein, a pornographic film director who conned one of the policeman into making an adult-oriented security system commercial. The new TWILIGHT ZONE series yielded him a cameo as a draft dodger unjustly sentenced to go to Hell. In HUNTER he made a walk-on appearance on the episode entitled "The Contract" as Vaughn.

1987 was a landmark year for Spiner. In two brief but memorable scenes in the TV movie FAMILY SINS, he played Ken McMahon, a sympathetic teacher of a troubled boy. As Bob Grand in an episode of CHEERS, he played a charismatic defendant who had been charged with attempting to murder his wife. He also put some time in on a couple of episodes of MAMA'S FAMILY, a show not known for its cerebral value. This he did in exchange for the promise of the significant role of Bob Wheeler, a very unlucky Yugoslavian hillbilly who showed up on six episodes of NIGHT COURT.

When Wheeler bought a snack bar in the courthouse, Spiner came close to acquiring his first regular job on a television series. And then he auditioned for a new series, winning the part of a golden hued android named Data. With the ensuing success of STAR TREK—THE NEXT GENERATION, Brent Spiner was catapulted into fame, gaining a large following of highly devoted fans.

When series creator Gene Roddenberry cast Spiner into the part of Data, the android's appearance was something not yet determined. Spiner went through 36 makeup tests, as makeup genius Michael Westmore painted him every color in the rainbow, including bubblegum pink and battleship gray. They finally settled upon bright gold, with yellow irised contacts.

Spiner was opposed to the idea of wearing makeup for his character at first. "My argument with Gene was, 'If you could make a creature that moves like this and looks like this and thinks like this, why can't you do the skin?' And Gene's response was, 'What makes you think what you have isn't better than skin?' And that's very difficult to argue with."

GOING BACK TO THE WELL

Roddenberry developed the character of Data from two previous sources. First, Data's childlike personality resembled that of the android found in the failed pilot of a series Roddenberry wrote entitled THE QUESTOR TAPES. Secondly, Data's desire to understand humans and their emotions corresponded to that of the Vulcan character Xon, whom Gene created in 1978 for the aborted STAR TREK II series.

In "Encounter at Farpoint," the pilot of STAR TREK—THE NEXT GENERATION, Riker refers to Data as "Pinocchio." Spiner uses this comparison in his portrayal of Data. "He's a machine who'd love to be human, and is fascinated by humans. I suppose in his journey he'll get closer and closer to being one."8 Another parallel can be drawn between Data and Roy Batty, the replicant played by Rutger Hauer in the movie BLADE RUNNER. "I like to think of myself as the Rutger Hauer of this show," Spiner revealed in an interview. "But then I like to think of myself as Rutger Hauer in real life: strikingly handsome, irresistible to women, an intergalactic enigma."

Spiner's self-image is not far from the truth, if female fan response to him is any indication. "The character who receives the most love letters on STAR TREK—THE NEXT GENERATION is the android Data. . . 'Quite a few want to know just how fully functional I really am. I'm assuming they mean my character.' . . . Spiner is sorting through the 50 marriage proposals he's received so far in the mail."

Spiner also won the devotion of the critics, many of whom otherwise panned the new series. "This is a clever android," wrote Lee Anne Nicholson. "Now if only some of it would rub off on the human characters. . . "

"Houstonian Brent Spiner is also strong as Lt. Cmdr. Data, the android whom many liken to the first cast's Mr. Spock," wrote Bruce Westbrook in his review of the series pilot. "But Data doesn't resist human qualities—he embraces them. And his innocent fence-straddling between man and machine provides most of the first episode's sly humor."

OUT OF THE LIMELIGHT

Despite this overwhelming attention, Spiner initially shied away from convention appearances and granted interviews only to Houston newspapers. He declined being photographed without Data makeup on and even requested that a fanzine devoted to him pull a pre-Trek photo of him from their first issue. "As much as people think they want to see me, they want to see Data," he explained in an interview. "The fact that I've become a cultural icon to some people—well, I love it, it excites me, and I don't want to disturb it. But I'm not going to fuel it, either."

However, he does admit that there is some of himself in Data: "A childishness. A childlike sense of wonder. . . With me, my emotional development was arrested around nineteen, so this allows me to be the child that I am."14 Unlike Data, however, Spiner has been noted by many co-workers for his wonderful sense of humor.

"[Brent] is so wonderful, funny and oddly enough very warm and human," said guest star Michelle Phillips in an interview. "I couldn't help but laugh every time I saw him in that lime color makeup he wears. . . I know he's supposed to be an android without personality, but he's a very funny character with a lot of personality."

Because his work on the show required Spiner to do a lot of acting in front of a blue screen (a cinematic device used to key in special effects in the background), he developed a new technique of acting called "Spining." This same technique has been used extensively by his fellow cast members. A great deal of camaraderie among the regular cast members developed quickly and they gave Spiner the nickname "Zippy the Android."

LONG DAYS

Part of what drove them closer together were the grueling hours they put into each day on the set, which can be anywhere from 12 to 17 hours by Spiner's estimate. Despite their exhausting, time-consuming schedules, the cast seemed able to keep up their energy. "We are probably the most raucous cast in Hollywood," Spiner said at a convention. "It's very much like a big night club on the bridge. . . It really gets so loud and so wild it's like we're doing a long improv all day long that's only broken up by having to do scenes for the show."

Extra James Becker had this to say: "Every day when Spiner and Frakes are running around, it's like a two-man comedy show. They are so funny, and they bring so much life to the set and keep so many people in good spirits. . . If they were gone, the tone would be much lower, and not too many people would laugh during the day. Those two know that it's all serious, but they keep a

light undertone so that the rest of us always feel this is gonna be fun."

Despite his schedule, Spiner's professional life was still extant outside of THE NEXT GENERATION. He appeared briefly in two movies directed by long-time friend and former schoolmate Tommy Schlamme. The first of these was MISS FIRECRACKER (1989) which yielded Spiner a cameo of Preacher Mann. The other was CRAZY FROM THE HEART (1991), a made-for-TV movie in which Spiner played a member of a school board. He also appeared on television in Billy Crystal's series SESSIONS (for cable channel HBO), in WHAT'S ALAN WATCHING? as Brentwood Carter, and in a rather humorous skit on cable channel Movietime.

Spiner has continued to impress people with his extraordinary acting abilities, including co-star Patrick Stewart, a man also highly praised for his own considerable talent. Stewart was particularly impressed with Spiner's performance in the episode "Datalore" in which he played not only Data, but Data's evil twin "brother," Lore. "[Brent] was so good that I was excited to be watching it," said Stewart. "You know, here's a man that I've worked with for eight or nine months who continues to go on impressing and surprising me."

GIVING IN

In response to continued pressure from fans and fellow cast members alike, Spiner finally succumbed to appearing at his first convention. The event happened at the Penta Hotel in New York on November 24-25, 1989. Those in attendance noticed that Spiner seemed to be quite nervous at first, which was quite natural, but he soon won them over with his graceful charm, sharp wit and mellow tenor singing voice.

Unfortunately, vicious—and to this date, unsubstantiated—rumors about

Spiner's behavior at the con rippled throughout the world of fandom. Not long after, he canceled a planned appearance at a convention in New Zealand, due to scheduling conflicts with the studio at which he was recording "Ol' Yellow Eyes is Back." It was not until almost two years later that Spiner again agreed to appear at conventions. He has since made several more appearances.

Even when appearing at these conventions, Spiner has been generally reticent about his personal life. "The only things I don't want to talk about are STAR TREK and my personal life," he (jokingly) tells con attendees at the beginning of each appearance. He declines requests for him to sing, due to lack of preparation. As Spiner has said, he doesn't do anything without rehearsing.

This importance of quality and pride in his work shows. He also tends to joke in order to avoid answering questions of a more personal or sensitive matter to him. For example, in response to a question about his age, he responded, "Have you ever noticed that when somebody takes a long pause that what they say after the pause is hardly worth .the wait? . . . I'm not going to tell you exactly how old I am, but. . . it's only in recent years that I've begun to understand what a real genius Jack Benny really was."

KEEPING IT PRIVATE

Little is actually known of his personal life. But he has revealed that he is single and has never been married, nor does he intend to marry while he is still on the show (he's too busy). There are those who like to pry, however. A photograph of Brent with co-star Whoopi Goldberg appeared in the NATIONAL ENQUIRER, inaccurately dubbing him "business exec Brent Spiner." He and Goldberg—both big fans of classic movies—were attending the

American Movie Awards, at which Spiner met some of his childhood idols, including Gene Autry and Clayton Moore (a.k.a. The Lone Ranger).

Spiner, who turned 43 in 1992, believes that Data is really a comedic character appearing in a dramatic series. The actor found it particularly funny that in the 1992 season cliffhanger, Data lost his head. "We didn't play it as if it were comical, but there is something comical about discussing losing your head."

Comedy is what attracted Spiner to the field of acting, in particular the comedy of Lucille Ball. "If there is any reason that I decided to become an actor it was the episode of I LOVE LUCY when she met William Holden at the Brown Derby. I watched the episode and I thought, 'I got to get out to Hollywood,' . . . I thought, 'I have to do that. I have to hang out at the Beverly Hills Hotel and meet Harpo Marx.'

ANYTHING IS POSSIBLE

Season six of THE NEXT GENERATION is the final contract year for the actors and Spiner is uncertain what will happen beyond that. There is talk about a NEXT GENERATION feature film but nothing has been confirmed yet. Meanwhile, Spiner isn't concerned that life after THE NEXT GENERATION will lead to him being typecast as an actor. "I don't think there are a lot of android parts out there."

As for Spiner, anything is possible for the future. He seems to prefer television work, but hasn't ruled out A return to the stage. "I've done a lot of work before STAR TREK, including twenty-five plays in New York, and I'd have no problem going back to do twenty-five more."

LT. COMMANDER

MARINA SIRTIS - Headshot at a dinner party for the Jewish Television Telethon. Photo: © 1993 Ortega/Ron Galella Ltd.

"Of alien descent, Counselor Troi met an old friend when she transferred to the Enterprise. And then there's the matter of Troi's mother. . ."

CHAPTER 7

LT. COMMANDER DEANNA TROI SHIP'S COUNSELOR

Deanna Troi holds the position of counselor, a position that didn't exist during the time of the voyages of the first starship Enterprise 78 years before. In the 24th century it has been realized that the success of a starship's mission depends as much on efficiently functioning human relationships as it does on the vessel staying in one piece and having fully functional warp drive.

Counselor Troi is fully trained in human and alien psychology. When a starship encounters alien life forms, the counselor's role is second only to that of the Captain and Number One is making decisions on how to deal with the other life forms.

The world has changed much in the future and the crew of a starship actually welcomes the insights of a ship's Counselor, even when it deals with an individual's own behavior and level of performance. While 20th century psychiatry and psychology is considered to be more of an art than an empirical science, in the 24th century solid evidence and medical research have radically changed things.

Psychiatry has become a field of applied science in which hard evidence has replaced guesswork, supposition and mere practiced insight. Command ranks aboard starships both respect and actively make use of the skills of the Counselor in much the same way that they solicit advice from the medical officers, chief engineer and other shipboard specialists. With the commissioning of the Galaxy Class starships, with the added complexities of families and the presence of children, the Counselor is in even more demand.

One of the rare people who serve as "focal points" in Federation history. Born into one of the oldest and richest houses of Betazed, (The Fifth House) and a member of aristocratic nobility (Holder of the Sacred chalice of Riix.) Her father, Ian Andrew, died when she was a child. Her mother, Lwaxana, smothered her with tradition, until the arrival of a young second officer on Betazed altered her life forever. Will Riker opened her eyes to the wide-open galaxy (and taught her to rebel against her mother's control).

ATTENDING STARFLEET

Deanna traveled to Earth, and even though it is not required for counselors, she insisted on attending command school and eventually rose to the rank of Lt. Commander. Her Terran father's influence on her biology led her to inherit empathic powers, yet not full telepathic powers such as her mother possesses.

A Starfleet graduate, Deanna is half human and half Betazoid. Her father was a Starfleet officer who lived on Betazed with one of that world's humanoid females. Her mother Lwaxana is an aristocratic eccentric who provides Deanna with acute embarrassment whenever she appears on board the Enterprise, since she seems insistent on pursuing Captain Picard (she thinks he has great legs), or whatever other male she sets her eyes on.

While Lwaxana and all other full Betazoids are fully telepathic, Deanna has telepathic abilities limited to the emotional range; she can "read" feelings and sensations, but not coherent thoughts. Another extreme example of Betazoid ability is the hyper-sensitive Tam Elbrun, who vanished with the space faring being dubbed "Tin Man" by the Federation. While most Betazoids develop their full telepathic abilities during adolescence, Elbrun was born with them fully functional, which led to extreme problems for him, leading him to seek the solitude of space. He was, in fact, Deanna's patient at one time, but she was not able to do much for him.

Due to her particular training and inherent abilities, Counselor Troi is often selected as an Away Team member as she can provide important insights into the motives and feelings of the beings they must deal with. (Some beings, notably the Ferengi, are impervious even to full telepaths. While some races may be able to intentionally block their minds, the Ferengi probably are resistant due to peculiarities of their brain structure.)

RELATIONSHIPS COUNT

Generally, when dealing with alien life, Deanna can sense something of the moods or attitudes that a being harbors toward the Federation representatives. In the case of the Traveler ("Where No One Has Gone Before") she could detect nothing from him, as if he wasn't even there. With humans she is able to sense more when it is a person she has some sort of rapport or relationship with.

For instance, while Troi was acquainted with William Riker before either was posted to the Enterprise, neither knew the other had been assigned to this starship until they first encountered one another on board. While Troi had not become deeply involved with Riker, she did find their affair meaningful and pleasant. It has not progressed any further as each feels honor bound to maintain a disciplined and professional status while aboard ship.

Deanna was given away as a child to be wed and was stunned to find her fiancé was going to arrive on her new ship. He, instead, sacrificed his freedom to help the members of a dying race, who had somehow called him to them at Haven. She realizes how having Will as her Imzadi will complicate relationship for both of them. She is trapped in a shuttlecraft by the entity Armus, who later kills Tasha Yar. Troi felt Yar die. Picard was able to use her guidance to outsmart and trap the deadly "oil slick."

Deanna once gave birth to a strange, alien son, whom she named Ian Andrew after she was impregnated by an unknown entity. The birth was painless and highly accelerated. The child's life was also brief. He returned to his natural energy state to protect the ship from destruction. She still misses him. She has recently helped Worf raise his son, Alexander, often helping the Klingons to learn to compromise.

DEAD AGAIN

Deanna's place in galactic history involves a plot from the future to assassinate her. [See IMZADI by Peter David.] In fact, she really did die. Once. A Sindareen plot to kill her was thwarted by an admiral she once knew. Before she died, an alien assassin traveled through the Guardian of Forever to kill Troi. He poisoned her and she died.

The first time through the time-line, she had exposed a Sindareen plot and prevented a win over the Federation. When she died, history shifted. Commodore Data noticed this, in the alternate time line 40 years in the future and confided this to Admiral Riker, who had lived with a broken heart for the alternate 40 years. Once he is determined it was a killer from the future, Riker left against orders to find Deanna and save her.

Only when he finds and protects her does the time-line reform around them. So the first time through, she lives. The second time, she died. The third time, she lives. She is, in fact, a reverse Edith Keeler. Edith had to die to allow the U.S. to win World War II, which would ultimately lead to the start of the Federation of Planets. By dying before she could alert Picard of the threat, Federation was altered. However, in the future, this was known.

Deanna once lost her powers and had to use instinct to help save the ship. She has had a series of short romances and continues her long-term Imzadi relationship with Will. Deanna continues to redefine her image and has taken to wearing a medical blue uniform, since Captain Jellico expressed displeasure over her informal attire.

Troi loves chocolate passionately and also enjoys poker, and tales of the "Ancient West." Troi is an expert on alien psychology, much as Beverly is an expert on alien physiology.

CHAPTER 8

MARINA SIRTIS

Born to Greek parents in North London, Marina demonstrated an inclination towards performing at an early age. "My mother tells me that when I was three, I used to stand up on the seat of the bus and sing to the other passengers." But her parents wanted their daughter to follow "more serious" pursuits, so after finishing high school, Marina had to secretly apply to the Guild Hall School of Music and Drama, where she was accepted. "My first job after graduating was as Ophelia in 'Hamlet' for the Worthing Repertory Company."

Following that, she worked for a few years in British television, musical theatre and in other repertory companies throughout England and Europe. She landed some supporting roles in features such as THE WICKED LADY (topless fight with Faye Dunaway over whip), in DEATHWISH III with Charles Bronson and BLIND DATE with Kirstie Alley. She's also completed the BBC film ONE LAST CHANCE and appears in a cameo in the horror-spoof WAXWORK II.

A British actress, Marina Sirtis had been working in various roles in England for years before she decided to give the colonies a try, but she landed the continuing role of Deanna Troi after being in America only six months. "It's taken me years to become an overnight success," she quips. "I had a six-month visa, which was quickly running out. In fact, I got the call telling me I had the part only hours before I was to leave for the airport to return home."

She decided to stay on in the United States and has settled in Los Angeles where she watches "far too much MTV" and keeps track of her local soccer team in London, in which she owns a few shares. Her brother is a professional soccer player.

A LOT TO DEAL WITH

Marina enjoys the irony of being a British actress playing an alien on American television. But viewers won't notice a British accent coming out of an alien being as she's devised a combination of accents for the character to use.

"In the 24th Century, geographical or nationalistic barriers are not so evident. The Earth as a planet is your country, your nationality. I didn't want anyone to be able to pin down my accent to any particular country, and being good at accents, the producers trusted me to come up with something appropriate, Sirtis states.

Sirtis initially auditioned for the role of Security Chief Tasha Yar, rather than that of Deanna Troi.

"After my third audition for Tasha, I was literally walking out the door when they called me back to read for Deanna. While I was looking at the script, director Corey Allen came in and said, 'You have something personally that the character should have. . . an empathy, so use it.' I love being able to play someone who is so deep with that kind of insight into people, particularly since I usually get cast as the hard 1980s stereotype."

But she had mixed feelings when first seeing her character on the screen. "I watched the pilot with my hands over my eyes. I didn't feel it was working. I got some really good feedback from people, but personally, knowing what I can do as an actress and what was up there, I wasn't really happy. I was really pleased to make changes. I personally thought that if

I continued to play Troi that way, it would get really boring because if you're telepathic, a psychologist, who is hugely super intelligent and has that kind of background, she would be so understanding, so nice, so forgiving, so laid back and perfect that I'd be the Linda Evans of STAR TREK. What I wanted more of was Alexis."

FINDING HER WAY

Like most characters on STAR TREK—THE NEXT GENERATION, Deanna Troi went through some rough passages during the first season, particularly when she almost got locked into the role of "sensing" things vital to plot development without having much further dimension as a character.

"They had dug that hole for themselves with me being an empathy," observed Sirtis in 1988, "[and] I nearly fell into it and was covered over." Apparently the show's writers went through a period where they were more than a bit uncertain as to what direction to take Deanna in. They even dropped her from some episodes, such as "11001001," "Heart of Glory," "Datalore" and "Hide & Q." In fact, some scenes with Deanna were actually trimmed from the script of "Hide & Q," among other episodes in order to cut back on casting expenditures.

She was even almost dropped from the cast halfway through the first season. Her contract certainly did not require her to be in every episode, and losing the character was considered, but fortunately a new contract for the second season strengthened her position and guaranteed her return.

And a good thing, too, as the character is greatly favored by fans of the series. Oddly enough, however, Marina Sirtis is not always recognized in public.

This is understandable in the case of Brent Spiner and even more so in the case of Michael Dorn, but is somewhat peculiar in that Sirtis' character make-up consists primarily of her hair style (which has been through a few changes during the course of six seasons) and a pair of dark contact lenses to cover her naturally green eyes.

In fact, many fans failed even to realize that the half-Betazoid Deanna Troi's dark, almost black eyes were a trait resulting from her alien background until her mother, Lwaxana (portrayed by Majel Barrett) appeared in the episode "Haven" and gave viewers a chance to notice that the two characters shared the trait of dark, almost pupil-less eyes.

TWO GOOD ONES

Despite the writing staff's lack of a grip on the character of Deanna during the first season, Marina Sirtis still fondly recalls working on two first season episodes. These were "Haven," which as noted, introduced us to her mother and gave us a bit more insight into her background, and "Skin of Evil," the episode wherein Tasha Yar was dispatched to her premature demise. Sirtis felt that she did some of her best work in "Skin of Evil." In that episode she and the other actors had to react to the death of Tasha Yar.

Sirtis regarded Yar's holographic farewell to her crewmates, "One of the most moving things we've ever shot." She noted that Denise Crosby actually shot one more episode, "Symbiosis," after "Skin of Evil," which made for an odd situation on the set of that episode. But in "Skin of Evil," Crosby spoke her lines off stage in the hologram scene. "Jonathan [Frakes] and I were standing together at that point," recalled Sirtis, "and I was sobbing. . . unfortunately, I started sobbing which got Jonathan very teary-eyed and set the tone.

Every time Denise looked at me, she just walled up because I was so sad that this was happening. I cried all day. No matter how many times I heard Denise do [the lines], no matter how many takes, it still made me cry."

But with the first season out of the way and the second season begun, there was no need to fear for Deanna Troi's job security, as the very first episode of season two featured Troi in the pivotal role when she was impregnated by a space entity that wanted to experience humanity and so conceived itself as "The Child" which she bore in that episode. Mirina Sirtis was very much in the limelight in that episode, which finally gave her more to do than state that she's sensing hostility from an alien spaceship.

Marina got to show a stronger side to her character when Deanna taken over by a brutal alien criminal in the fifth season episode "Power Play." Then we saw Troi become a truly dangerous personality. Most changes in her character, though have been superficial. For instance, her hair style changed from the awful 24th century beehive of season one to the more attractive look she wears now. Her uniform, which has always been somewhat lackluster, was suddenly changed to a regular command uniform in "Chain Of Command" when Picard's replacement ordered her to dress like everyone else. Interestingly, she was seen to be still wearing this uniform in subsequent episodes after Picard had returned.

ROOM TO GROW

Marina Sirtis, along with other NEXT GENERATION actors such as Jonathan Frakes, has continued to be critical of the show's portrayal of women characters. Although great strides have been taken since the days of tinfoil miniskirts which marked the original STAR TREK, the new series still falls flat on its face as far as modern women are concerned, and its moral and ethical views are still rooted several decades in our past.

Such controversies aside, Marina Sirtis continues as a vital part of THE NEXT GENERATION's crew. Since those early days, she had been well utilized in numerous episodes, both as support and in the foreground. And, like many members of the cast, Marina Sirtis enjoys attending conventions. "I love doing conventions," she confesses," because I have a great time on stage in front of the audience. I would hate to get up there and not be responded to, but I do get a response. It gives me the thrill of a stage performance without having to learn any lines! Some actors forget that however talented you are, it's the public that made you popular."

Regarding what it's like working with her fellow actors on the series, she states, "We've always had fun. All the directors have said they've never worked on such a fun set. It's incredible to have actors who get along so well. It's so cliche, but we're all so happy to be here."

Marina has always been interested in the stars and space exploration and believes that she once saw a UFO. "I was working with a repertory company in Worthing, a seaside town in England. One night as I was walking down the street, I saw this huge orange thing in the sky. At first I thought it must be the moon, but it was very off color. It was very close, but too high to be a balloon. Apparently a lot of other people saw it, too."

An ardent feminist, she credits NEXT GENERATION with allowing her to keep a visa and to live and work in the U.S. "I always act for free," she once remarked. "They pay me for waiting around."

Obviously untainted by any touch of arrogance, it's a sure bet that Marina Sirtis will be working long after STAR TREK—THE NEXT GENERATION takes its place in history.

LIEUTENANT

Levar Burton - Headshot at the wedding of Marina Sirtis.

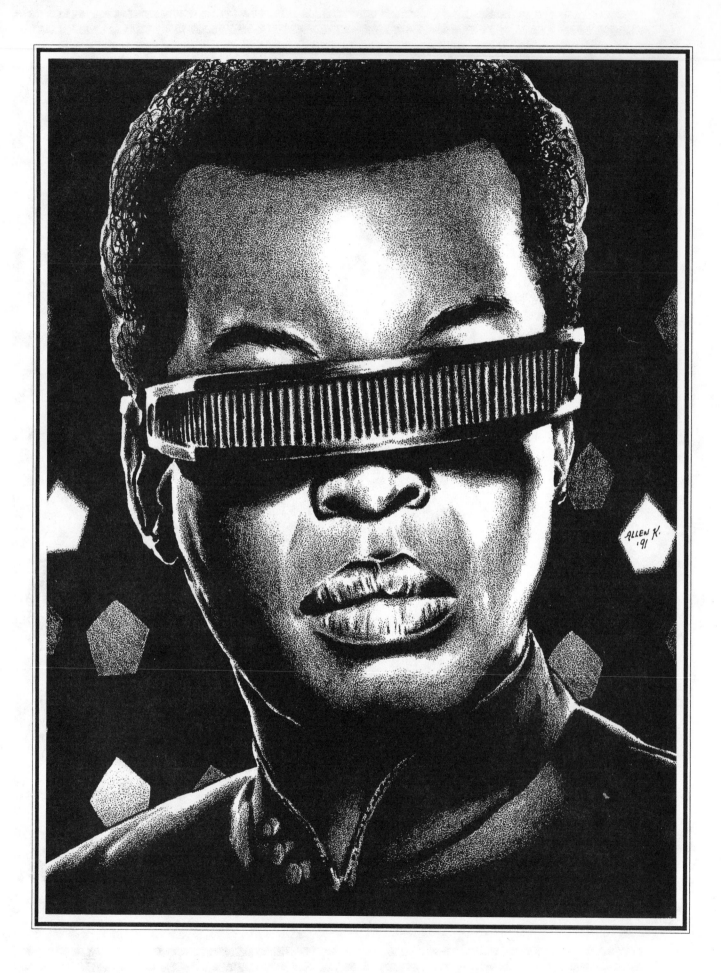

> *"The Enterprise Chief Engineer is his own man and is anything but a carbon copy of Montgomery Scott."*

CHAPTER 9

LT. J.G. GEORDI LA FORGE

By Alex Burleson

Geordi LaForge was born blind and is one of four Starfleet officers able to wear a VISOR band for sight. Most visually impaired officers rely on webbed sensor sets. (VISOR— VISUAL INSTRUMENT AND SIGHT ORGAN REPLACEMENT). Geordi is both trained to work on the bridge and is an away team regular whose unique prosthetic eyes allow him to perform some of the functions of a tricorder.

His high-tech artificial eyes can detect the entire spectrum of electromagnetic waves, all the way from raw heat to high-frequency ultraviolet. Other crew persons seem blind by comparison. Although Geordi sometimes wishes he could see the way they do, he once rejected the opportunity to be permanently given human sight by Q when the entity was offered it to him.

Both of Geordi's parents were Starfleet officers. His mother was a command officer assigned to patrol the Romulan Neutral Zone. His father was a xenozoologist stationed in the Modine System. He was always on the move between the two. As a child he was traumatized by a fire since his blindness prevented him from knowing how to escape it. His parents rescued him, but those moments he felt helpless was an experience he'll never forget.

LaForge was assigned to Navigation on the USS Victory after he graduated Starfleet Academy. He then transferred to the USS Hood (where he first met Will Riker), before being promoted to serve on the Enterprise.

Geordi's commitment to his duties was aptly demonstrated to his Captain when LaForge had taken Picard on an inspection tour in a shuttle. There Picard made an off-hand reference to the shuttle's efficiency. When Picard found out that Geordi had stayed up all night refitting the fusion initiators just due to the Captain's off-hand remark, he requested Geordi's presence on the Federation flagship Enterprise.

WISDOM BEYOND HIS YEARS

Although in his early twenties, Geordi has the maturity of a seasoned Starfleet graduate and has the highest respect for Captain Picard, hoping to emulate the Captain when he gets older. His best friend aboard the Enterprise is the android Data. Each aspires to be "fully human," because even though they have traits that make them superior in what they can achieve compared to their normal counterparts, neither asked to be different, nor wants to be. Perhaps Geordi needs an intensive therapy session with Counselor Troi in order to accept himself for what he is so that he can more readily get on with his life.

LaForge is credited with the "LaForge Maneuver" for his heroic efforts against an alien weapons system in orbit of Minos. Picard left LaForge in command, so Geordi deftly handled superior officers and nervous ensigns to enter the planet's atmosphere, using the heat of re-entry to neutralize the cloaking device that protected the weapon. After the rescue, Picard insists that Geordi retain command until the saucer section is attached.

Geordi and a Romulan worked together to survive an electrical storm on Galandan Kor and prevent a Romulan attack on the Enterprise. When the Enterprise is threatened by an ancient boobytrap, he creates a holodeck character with the personality of Dr. Leah Brahms, then falls in love with her. When the real Dr. Brahms arrives, Geordi is heartbroken to find out she is nothing like his "holodeck Leah," And married, no less.

Geordi found himself transformed into an alien entity when an Away Team he was once on was infected by an alien program of reproduction—through human hosts. Geordi is transformed, but his friends convince him to return—in the nick of time.

Romulans once kidnapped Geordi on his way to a conference on artificial intelligence which was being held on Risea. He was very badly mistreated and conditioned to assassinate a Klingon governor, in a Romulan attempt to undermine the Klingon-Federation alliance. Data is able to realize what happened and warns Worf who is able to warn Picard in time to prevent the death.

The brainwashing of Geordi had been so effective that he believed he had attended the conference of Risea and was only subconsciously aware of the communications he made with the Klingon traitor who was his control in the assassination plot. While Troi was able to help him separate the real memories from the false thereafter, he still had to undergo counseling to overcome the trauma of the torture inflicted upon him by Sela's henchmen.

GONE BUT NOT FORGOTTEN

In one of his most amazing experiences, LaForge discovered the pattern of Captain Montgomery Scott in a Transporter which had been left in cycle in a ship stranded on a Dyson Sphere. (At one point he seemed to regret doing so.) After an initial friendship, Geordi snaps at Scott's impudence and angers the "Miracle Worker." Picard forces the two together and they wind up pulling off another miracle to rescue the Enterprise.

Geordi considers Data his best friend and treats him just the same as if he were human. "You're not just another machine!" "And you are not just another biological organism," Data replies.

When Geordi and Ro were presumed dead in a Transporter accident, Data planned the funeral. It proved premature when Geordi and Ro have actually suffered from a phase-shift which has altered their molecular structure (except for the floor, I guess) and they are returned to normal to the surprise of everyone at the "party."

Geordi became the first Terran to reach the Delta Quadrant when a wormhole took the shuttlecraft there during an experiment. They were looking for Gamma Quadrant. (DEEP SPACE NINE's Commander Benjamin Sisko is the first Terran to reach the Gamma Quadrant, 70,000 light-years away. Geordi was joined by Data—and Sisko by Jadzia Dax.)

LaForge enjoys varied holodeck programs, including: string musicians on a beach, historical settings, the Mars

Planetia Shipyards, a steaming hot bath, and Don Quixote programs.

Geordi served as Miles O'Brien's best man. Data gave away the bride. Geordi befriended diagnostician Reg Barclay and that has proved valuable on more than one occasion.

CHAPTER 10

LEVAR BURTON

By Alex Burleson

Due to the longevity of the original series, the new crew has more than one actor who was a STAR TREK fan before landing his role, and Levar Burton is one of them. He states that he has long "appreciated Gene Roddenberry's approach to science fiction. Gene's vision of the future has always included minorities—not just blacks, but Asians and Hispanics as well. He's saying that unless we learn to cooperate as a species, we won't be able to make it to the 24th Century. I think that by projecting that image, we're actually creating a reality for today.

"I liked the old show an awful lot," LeVar added, "and when I heard Gene Roddenberry was also doing this one it said to me that this show was also going to be done right, with taste, dignity and integrity. We have one of the best ensembles in the business. We all respect and admire each other."

Philosophy has long been an interest of Levar Burton. At 13 he entered a Catholic seminary, with the ultimate goal of becoming a priest. But after two years he discovered an interest in Existentialism and by 15 was reading Lao-Tzu, Kierkegaard and Nietzche.

"I began to wonder how I fit into the grand scheme of things. The more I thought about it, the less sense it made that the dogma of Catholicism was the end-all, be-all of the universe," Burton explains.

Following what Burton describes as his "pragmatic search," comparing the things he did well with the things that excited him about being a priest, he decided to pursue an acting career.

"What attracted me to the priesthood was the opportunity to move people, to provide something essential. I was drawn by the elements of history and magic. As a priest, you live beyond the boundaries of the normal existence. It's like joining an elite club. You see, it's not that different from acting, even the Mass is a play, combining these elements of mystery and spectacle."

MOVING ON

After he left the seminary, Burton won a scholarship to USC, where he began working toward a degree in drama and fine arts. But the contrast between the sedate, introspective life in a small town seminary and the USC campus, which he calls "Blond Central," was startling. "I'd never had so much freedom and it was difficult to concentrate the first year."

It was during his sophomore year at USC, while only 19, that he auditioned and landed the pivotal role of the young Kunta Kinte in the award-winning mini-series Roots.

"I think the producers had exhausted all the normal means of finding professional talent and were beating the bushes at the drama schools," the actor ventures. The role would win him an Emmy nomination and subsequent acting roles, which prevented his return to college.

Burton starred in a number of made-for-TV movies such as the Emmy-nominated DUMMY, ONE IN A MILLION: THE RON LeFLORE STORY, GRAMBLING'S WHITE TIGER,

THE GUYANA TRAGEDY: THE STORY OF JIM JONES, BATTERED, BILLY: PORTRAIT OF A STREET KID, ROOTS CHRISTMAS: KUNTE KINTE'S GIFT and the mini-series LIBERTY. The actor has also been the host of PBS' highly acclaimed children's series READING RAINBOW since its inception in 1983, which is a show he created and has written and directed. Both ROOTS and READING RAINBOW received multiple Emmy Awards. Among his film credits are LOOKING FOR MR. GOODBAR, a memorable turn in THE HUNTER (with the late Steve McQueen) and THE SUPERNATURALS (with Nichelle Nichols).

IT'S WHO YOU KNOW

The actor was born in Landsthul, West Germany, where his father was a photographer in the Signal Corps, Third Armored Division. His mother was first and educator, then for years a social worker who is currently working in administration for the County of Sacramento Department of Mental Health. Burton is single and resides in Los Angeles with his German Shepherd, Mozart.

A previous association with producer Robert Justman (a part on the series EMERGENCY ROOM) led to a tryout for the new program that Justman was working on with Gene Roddenberry. Burton's first audition for THE NEXT GENERATION was an interesting one: he knew that the character he was trying out for had been born blind but was unaware that the character would be able to see as a result of a device.

The VISOR had not yet been designed—the breakthrough would occur when a production designer adapted the design of his daughter's hair barrette to become the sight-giving device. In the interim, Burton tried out for the character by playing him as sightless. He had played

blind people before (including a role on THE LOVE BOAT!), but was informed that this would not be necessary for the role of LaForge.

During the first season of TNG, LeVar Burton felt somewhat at sea, as the character of Geordie LaForge did not really get much opportunity to develop. . . he was just a guy with a high-tech seeing aid. (Which, incidentally, Burton can see through, but only about seventy percent of his visual ability.) In fact, Burton claims to be unable to even remember much about the first season of the series, which says a lot about how little he was given to do during that first year.

PLAYING A BIGGER ROLE

With the second season, LaForge came into his own a bit more, being promoted to chief of engineering and being given the chance to get involved in both main plots and more personal subplots involving various relationships, such as that with Dr. Leah Brahms. Geordi's more crucial technical role meant, also, that whenever he appeared it helped to move the plot along; he was no longer merely taking up space on the set.

Soon, Geordi became one of the most prominently likable characters on the show, eternally optimistic but tinged with a tiny bit of healthy skepticism and just a touch of the happy cynic. A crucial development was the friendship which grew between Geordi and Data, a vital link for both characters in their development as people. All of this was aided immeasurably by the consummate skill of LeVar Burton the actor, described by one fellow cast member as doing the best "eyebrow acting" in the business.

The character Geordi LaForge is named after a disabled STAR TREK fan who passed away. The character of Geordi was created by David Gerrold.

In addition to his ongoing NEXT GENERATION work, LeVar Burton has been the host of PBS' READING RAINBOW series for the past decade, and he can also be heard contributing his vocal talents to the animated series CAPTAIN PLANET (along with Whoopi Goldberg). He is currently working on a project to star in and direct in South Africa.

Burton was quoted in NEW VOYAGES as saying: "When we make STAR TREK: THE NEXT GENERATION—THE MOTION PICTURE, I want the teaser to be Geordi loses his visor. I want to see again."

MICHAEL DORN - Headshot at Marina's wedding
Photo: © 1993 Ortega/Ron Galella Ltd.

The prediction made by the Organians nearly a century before has come to pass. The Klingon Empire and the Federation are at peace. Even so, Worf is unique as the only Klingon officer of a Starfleet ship.

CHAPTER 11

LIEUTENANT WORF

By Alex Burleson

Worf was named after his grandfather, who became widely known as the military colonel who served as defense attorney to James T. Kirk and Leonard McCoy when the two were accused of the assassination of Klingon Chancellor Gorkon.

Worf was born on the Klingon homeworld and soon left home with his natural parents who were ordered to Khitomer. The Romulan government was angry with the Klingon High Council over the recently signed Treaty of Alliance that bound the Klingons to the Federation. The thlIngan wo' had been long-time trading partners with the ch'Ri'han and ch'Havran (Romulus and Remus), and the Romulans ordered the attack as retaliation. It was a mass slaughter with few survivors. Worf was told that everyone died during the attack, but he later found that his nurse, Kahlest, had also survived, and the space station Deep Space Nine may play a part in Worf's future search.

In Peter David's novel STRIKE ZONE, Worf explained what had happened. He was in an attack shelter with his parents when the Romulans began a direct phaser attack on the colony from orbit. Worf indicated that his father was killed instantly and his mother moments later, after she shielded her young from the debris.

Worf was deeply traumatized by those events, and later in life he refused to give a Romulan a cellular transfusion that would have saved his life. Worf also developed a deep dislike for the Kreel. The Kreel salvaged what was left of the outpost. Worf could hear them as he lay under his mother's body amid the rubble. He finally dug an arm through to the surface, in time to hear a Starfleet officer shout: "Here's one!" He was pulled from the rocks by that officer and decided that the second he was "born again" during the rescue to dedicate his life to that organization.

A HUMAN FAMILY

Worf was adopted by Chief Petty Officer Sergei Rozhenko and his wife, Helena—a pair of Slavic farmers who loved the young Klingon as their own son. The Rozhenko's did their best to keep their adopted son in touch with his Klingon roots. He spent part of his youth on the farming world of Gault, before moving to Terra after Sergei retired.

On Earth, Worf immersed himself in Klingon culture and refused to eat any non-Klingon cuisine—forcing Helena to learn to cook Klingon-style. His favorite food was her Rokeg Blood Pie. He later remembered that this had been the last meal he had eaten with his family on

Kitomer. He had let his pet Targ taste it just before the raid sirens began. Worf began the first thlIngan (Klingon) applicant to Starfleet Academy, overcoming tremendous prejudice to become the first Klingon to enter Starfleet and gain officer's rank. Worf graduated second in his class at the Academy and

WORF'S ATTRIBUTE PROFILE

Strength—80
Intelligence—72
Endurance—70
Dexterity—69
Character—37
Luc—30
Psi Rating—09

Worf's primary language is Galactica (Standard)—80, yet he is fluent in Klingonese. Captain Picard did outscore him in the Klingon language 30-25.

Worf's strongest subjects in the Academy included:
Unarmed Person Combat—80
Armed Personal Combat—77
Klingon Psychology—67
Starship Security Procedures—55
Klingon History/Culture—55
Leadership—50
Small Unit Tactics—40
Computer Operation—33
Starship Navigation—33
Federation Culture/History—30

Worf's weakest scores were in:
Human General Medicine—10
Shuttlecraft Piloting—12
Federation Law—20
Warp Drive Technology—20
Starship Helm Operation—20
Computer Science—22
Human Psychology—22
Administration—28

delighted in proving his critics wrong. Worf's attribute profile is remarkable:

EARNED RESPECT

After Worf graduated he joined Starfleet, and was treated with the same courtesy and respect shown any other bridge officer—possibly even more, since the Klingons still have a remarkable reputation for violence. Although Worf is very aggressive by nature, he is able to control his anger even when he feels he has been provoked.

As a bridge officer, and the third in the line of command after Picard and Riker, Worf takes his duties very seriously. In combat situations, when the Enterprise or its crew are threatened, Worf wants to instinctively respond in kind and confront the menace head on.

Worf rarely talks about himself and his culture, but in "Justice" Riker inadvertently got Worf to talk about Klingon sexual attitudes. When Riker wonders why Worf is not enjoying the pleasures offered by the sybaritic Edo, Worf explains, quite casually, that only Klingon women could survive sex with a Klingon male. When Riker wonders if this is simply bragging, Worf is confused. He was merely stating a simple fact of Klingon life.

When Security Chief Tasha Yar died in the line of duty, Worf was chosen to succeed to command position as Security Chief of the USS Enterprise, the first Klingon to serve such a post.

When a crew member is killed by a device left by a long-dead race, Worf is frustrated because there is no one to take revenge against, and, while he obeys the orders of his superiors, he is not entirely at ease with the nonviolent solutions often dictated by Starfleet policy. The Klingon Empire does not stress cool deliberations as the preferred method for problem solving.

WORF AND HIS WOMEN

Worf had a brief affair with a Klingon named Gava. Her father, the Honorable Kobry, was the sole survivor of a separate Romulan attack and was educated and raised by Federation parents, returning home as an honored ambassador.

Worf also had a brief affair with a Klingon-Terran hybrid named K'Ehleyr. He did not see her again until years later when she was chosen Federation Emissary to deal with a crew of Klingons that had been in suspended animation since before the two cultures had allied. Worf served his first command of the Enterprise in negotiating the surrender of the ancient Klingon warship.

He and K'Ehleyr engaged in battle simulations in the holodeck and passion overwhelmed them. He offered to take the mating oath, yet K'Ehlyr did not believe it was necessary. She was concerned Worf was mating out of honor rather than love. As she transported to take control of the Klingon ship, Worf told her he would never be whole without her. A child was produced as she bore his son, Alexander, yet withheld the knowledge until she could tell him in person.

Worf was stunned when a Klingon exchange officer named Commander Kurn confessed to being his younger brother. Kurn had been left on the Klingon homeworld, since Moag did not expect the family to stay long on Khitomer. Kurn was raised by a friend of his father, who had no sons. He grew up to rise through the ranks to Klingon Captain.

Kurn was stunned to learn that his father had been declared a traitor. Upon hearing of his elder brother's exploits, Kurn decided to track Worf down and find

out if his heart was truly Klingon. After Worf passes the "anger" test ("I didn't want to hurt you.") Kurn admits his deception and calls on Worf to return with him to clear his name.

A KEY SPOKESMAN

Worf asks Picard for permission and upon finding out that Worf could be executed, decides to accompany him. Worf chooses Kurn as his Chadice, or second, and invites Picard and Riker to Join him. Picard speaks up for Worf before the high council just after a Duras' assassination attempt on Kurn, as Worf had chosen Picard to serve as Chadice. Data and Geordi are able to find out through computer records that Moag was innocent, and in fact it was Duras' father that betrayed the outpost.

Worf agrees to accept "discommendation" and dishonor in order to protect the Empire from civil war due to the support of the Duras family has on the High Council. The Leader of the High Council, K'mpec, decrees that Worf's name is not to be spoken again, even though he knows of the Duras' plot. Duras later is in a position to lead the Council after K'mpec is poisoned. Worf is convinced of Duras' complicity in the crime, but Picard is forced to arbitrate the selection of the leader. Duras once again tries assassination, but his plan backfires when he uses a molecular decay detonator which can be traced to the Romulans.

K'Ehlyr serves as Picard's Klingon Law expert and Worf is stunned to learn that he has a son. He refuses to claim him since that would mean Alexander must bear his family disgrace as well. He already insisted Kurn concealed his true identity. He begins to take the mating oath with K'Ehlyr, but breaks it off because he is concerned about discrediting her in the eyes of the Empire. She begins to unravel Duras' trail of lies and is killed in a fight over a knife.

She identifies her assailant and dies in Worf's arms, holding Alex's hand. Worf expurgates a Klingon death yell, warning 2 second in the ritual, also according to strict Klingon custom. But Worf could not bring himself to force such a trauma on the child. Worf agreed to try an extremely risky operation, but it seems to fail and he's pronounced legally dead when he suffers a complete synaptic failure. As Troi and Alexander grieve, Worf goes into convulsions as his second synaptic system kicks in.

Klingons are remarkably sturdy as evolution has gifted the warrior race with an eight-chambered heart, two kidneys and several redundant life support systems. Worf immediately began physical therapy to recover the use of his legs, which proceeded admirably, and Worf even allowed his son to participate in helping him.

In one incident, when the Enterprise crew suffers complete memory loss of their individual identities, Worf assumes temporary command of the Enterprise in belief that he must be Captain as he's the only Klingon aboard. When the crew learns the truth, Worf apologizes to Picard for his presumption.

A LINK TO UNDERSTANDING

Worf was honored with Starfleet's highest honor for bravery, above and beyond the call of duty, for his skillful leadership of a battalion in battle on Cantos V. Worf initially tried to turn it down since as a Klingon he thought there was no such thing as "above and beyond" the call of duty. He later decided there was

a difference between pride and mere foolish pride.

When Data was feared dead in a shuttlecraft explosion, Picard and Riker chose Worf to move up to Ops. He was relieved to return to tactical which he considers his true calling. Worf has also been known to override the mortality failsafe when working out on the holodeck in combat simulations. Worf is typical of Imperial Klingons in height, weight and strength. His physiognomy is also classically Klingon, distinctive for his family line. He has brown eyes and brown hair and was 38 years old at the time he was profiled in NEXT GENERATION'S OFFICER'S MANUAL.

Worf enjoys love poetry and build's model ships as a hobby. He prefers to work two shifts at a time and has been known to serve as many as eighty consecutive hours on the bridge during battle situation, and Picard must often order him off the bridge.

It seems that Worf may turn out to be a key factor in Klingon/ Federation relations. Klingons as a rule do not feel comfortable with humans, often holding them in contempt, and there may be a faction (see "The Drumhead") which favors improved relations with the Romulans; even though Klingons have a deeply ingrained hatred of Romulans, they understand them better than humans, whose manners and motivations often must seem strange to the warrior Klingons. Worf occupies a unique position between these two cultures, and may provide the key to future developments between them.

CHAPTER 12

MICHAEL DORN

By Alex Burleson

Dorn hails from Liling, Texas, but he was raised in Pasadena, California, just minutes away from Hollywood. He attended Pasadena City College to study psychology, but found that it wasn't for him. Instead he switched his career goals to producing radio and television. He performed in a rock band during high school and college and in 1973 moved away to San Francisco where he worked at a variety of jobs. When he returned to L.A., he continued playing in rock bands until a friend's father, an assistant director of THE MARY TYLER MOORE SHOW, suggested the young man try his hand at acting. Dorn can be seen in the background, as a news writer, in episodes from that classic comedy's last two seasons.

"I had done a little modeling by this time and had studied drama and TV producing in college. Once I started, I caught the bug." In college he had intended to work behind the camera only, but since college stations are small and everyone has to pitch in, he found himself sometimes called upon to do some acting. His work in front of the camera was impressive enough that he was advised to pursue it more seriously.

His first acting role was a guest spot on the series WEB, a show based on the satirical film NETWORK. Dorn was introduced to an agent by the producer of the show and began studying with Charles Conrad. Six months later Dorn was cast in CHiPS, where he worked for three years as Ponch and Jon's seldom-used back-up. Following that series, Dorn resumed acting classes. "I worked very hard; the jobs started coming and the roles got meatier."

Dorn has made guest appearances on nearly every major series, most notably HOTEL, KNOTS LANDING, FALCON CREST and PARKER LEWIS CAN'T LOSE. He has also had recurring roles on DAYS OF OUR LIVES and CAPITOL. On the series DINOSAURS he was heard as the voice of "The Cave of the Elders." His feature film credits include DEMON SEED, ROCKY and JAGGED EDGE. Dorn was a co-star in STAR TREK VI: THE UNDISCOVERED COUNTRY in which he played Worf's grandfather. This makes Dorn the first NEXT GENERATION actor to appear in a STAR TREK motion picture.

WORDS OF PRAISE

As a longtime STAR TREK fan, Dorn says that this role "was a dream come true. First, because I'm a Trekkie and second, I'm playing a Klingon, a character so totally different from the nice-guy roles I'd done in the past. Worf is the only Klingon aboard the Enterprise. That still makes him an outsider, but that's okay by me because Worf knows he's superior to these weak humans. But he never lets the other crew members see that because he's a soldier first and second."

The actor gives enthusiastic praise to series creator Gene Roddenberry for having the "genius and vision" to depict an optimistic future in which a peaceful alliance could be struck between Earth and the Klingon Empire. "Gene believes there is good in everybody—even Klingons!"

Dorn also appreciates the fact that the actors are allowed input in the scripts. "We have a script meeting and that's when we go through everything. For example, in one scene Worf, the consummate warrior, is stalking these soldiers and when the battle comes I dodge one bayonet and trip. I said if this guy is the consummate warrior, he doesn't trip on a rock. They go, 'You're right' and change it."

The key episode in the first season which broadened and deepened the character of Worf was certainly "Heart Of Glory." Regarding this story, Dorn states, "I consider 'Heart of Glory' to be an information episode because it gives you everything you wanted to know about what happened with the Klingons. Why did they become allies? Why is Worf there? How did he get there? That type of thing. It was very good, although I felt it could have been taken a little further. What I wanted was an epic battle at the end, but it was a good show for me because it showed them that people are as interested in Worf as they are in the other characters."

ADVANTAGES

Dorn enjoys playing very different kinds of characters, and knows what its like to appear in a series after playing a regular on CHiPS for three years. "I love doing cop roles, and as a highway patrolman I got to drive fast and I never got hurt."

The actor appreciated the advantages of doing a show aimed at the syndication market as opposed to the networks, and stated so right at the beginning of the series run. "We're already into shows dealing with certain situations you couldn't do on a network. In this day

and age of AIDS, networks have a responsibility. They're umbilically tied to their sponsors, but we're not under that type of gun and that's really nice. . . Really nice!"

During his first season on THE NEXT GENERATION, Dorn would sometimes enter the stage without his makeup and a director or producer would fail to recognize him and question what he was doing there. This was because the elaborate makeup Dorn has to put on requires him to arrive on the lot long before most of the cast and crew arrive and by the time the prosthetics are removed at the end of the day, most everyone else has already left.

"The anonymity is great," Dorn told the L.A. TIMES, "and I like the effect it has on people when I tell them who I am. But there's that ten percent of the actor that would love to be recognized." Once in awhile someone will recognize his voice, which is an unmistakable deep baritone. "They hear the voice and say, 'Do I know you? Who are you?' And when I tell them, they're floored."

ONE STEP AT A TIME

Dorn hopes eventually to direct, but for now, "I want to take one step at a time and do the best work I can do." He's still interested in rock music, plays in a band, does studio work as a bass player and writes music in his spare time.

Dorn's distinctive baritone was recently heard on Public Broadcasting's STORYTIME series for children. There Dorn read "The Little Red Hen" as well as the more recent children's tale "Company's Coming," a tale of aliens who arrive for dinner. "Anything that has to do with kids is for me," Dorn explains. "Children are our hope for the future and our country seems to neglect that."

GATES MCFADDEN - Headshot at the Bonaventure Convention.

Photo: © 1993 Ortega/Ron Galella Ltd.

"Chief Medical Officer Beverly Crusher (who bears a somewhat unfortunate last name for a practitioner of the healing arts) has demonstrated a grasp of a wide range of 24th century medicine, including xenobiology."

CHAPTER 13

DR. BEVERLY CRUSHER

By Alex Burleson and James Van Hise

Beverly's family survived the tragic devastation of a Federation colony at Alvega III. Her grandmother taught her to use herbal remedies which led to her interest in medicine. She never considered becoming a full Starfleet officer, yet knew the Starfleet Medical Academy was the best training a young doctor could receive. She first visited Earth to arrive at Starfleet Medical in San Francisco. There she met, and fell in love with, a young Starfleet officer named Jack Crusher.

Crusher served aboard the USS Stargazer, captained by a brash young captain named Jean-Luc Picard. She remained on Earth and Jack would send tapes back to tell her of his exploits. On one extended leave, young Wesley Crusher was conceived. Beverly first met Jean-Luc Picard when he was 40. After graduating from the Medical Academy, Beverly set up a private practice in San Francisco, doing research into multi-species medicine and space medicine.

Eight years later, her life changed forever. Jean-Luc Picard returned to Terra to bring back the body of his best friend. There are two versions of Jack's death. In the novel REUNION, Michael Jan Friedman suggests Crusher was killed while trying to detach a warp nacelle. But in David Gerrold's earlier novel (and the first TNG book) ENCOUNTER AT FARPOINT, he suggests Jack was killed by natives on an Away mission. Both reports indicate that Picard risked his life to retrieve the body. To show his respect for the man, Picard accompanied the body back to Earth when it was returned for the funeral.

When Beverly is later "mentally raped" by an Eulian, he forces her to relive a nightmarish view of the event of Picard and Jack's return.

THE RIGHT THING

The day after Jack died, Beverly enlisted as a Starfleet Medical Officer. She knew how much Jack loved Starfleet. Years later when she noticed that the USS Enterprise was being staffed, she volunteered for the posting and she and Wes left the USS Hood to rendezvous with the Enterprise at Farpoint Station on Deneb IV. When Picard first approaches her, he offers to have her transferred off his ship. He did not realize she had volunteered to serve with the man who held himself responsible for her husband's death.

While Beverly knows that it is not logical to blame Picard, she associated him with her loss and was not, at first, certain how she would react to working with Picard. When Picard offered to have her transferred, she declined, since she wouldn't have been there if she hadn't requested the position. Any initial misgivings have given way to mutual respect and understanding.

While bonding her with Jean-Luc, that and the natural captain-doctor relationship kept their mutual attraction from maturing into a full romance. Although she was once wooed by a doppelganger of Picard, who took his place at dinner, Dr. Crusher does not often share breakfast or other meals with the Captain. In fact he will usually ask her if an event even requires an escort. A running joke is that every time Beverly starts to tell Picard how she really feels, a major crisis develops, from Picard disappearing into thin air to terrorist attack.

Dr. Crusher chose to sign aboard the starship commanded by Picard because she has an enviable Starfleet record which has earned her this prestigious assignment. As demonstrated by the position held by Dr. McCoy on the Enterprise commanded by James T. Kirk, a starship's Chief Medical Officer is in no way regarded as a rank inferior to that of Captain. In fact, outside of a court martial, the CMO is the only force capable of removing a starship captain from his or her post.

SKILLS AND TRUTHS

Beverly is an intelligent and strong-willed diagnostician. She has a profound sense of medicine, the kind of skill that takes years to develop. Often she uses her diagnostic skills to confirm what she has already seen, smelled and sensed about a patient's condition. First and foremost she is a brilliant ship's doctor.

In "The Naked Now" there were many truths revealed about various crew members. In Crusher's case it revealed that she is interested in Picard, and certainly no longer harbors the suspicion and resentment she feared might affect her job performance. Being in her late thirties to early forties, the attractive Dr. Crusher has not escaped the notice of Captain Picard, but it is doubtful that this could develop into anything as any good officer knows that complications arise when key personnel become involved.

Dr. Crusher's most difficult moments on the Enterprise generally involve Wesley, as in "Justice" when Wesley was sentenced to death for an inadvertent crime, only to be saved by Picard's intervention.

Her most difficult time with Wesley occurred in "The First Duty" when Wesley narrowly escaped death in a training exercise off Saturn, in which another cadet did die. She was stunned to hear of Wesley's accident, yet relieved to find out that he was not injured, and proud that he made the right decision. Her son admitted to participating in a cover-up of the accident.

Beverly became the first person stranded in an alternate warp bubble when she walked into one of Wesley's experiments. She was able to reason out the problem and facilitate Wes's rescue efforts. When the ship was trapped in a causality loop, she was the first to recognize the time-loop. Beverly acts in the ship's recreational drama department and directs the casts and the productions.

DANCING AND ROMANCING

She enjoys exercising with Deanna, and has been seen in the ship's "Beauty Parlor." She also plays poker and is one of the best dancers in the Federation. A point she has downplayed since becoming known as "The Dancing Doctor." She has extraordinary medical standards and was promoted to the position of Chief Medical Officer of Starfleet Medicine. While honored, she found she missed the fieldwork and felt overwhelmed by the paperwork and bureaucracy. She also is an exobotonist in her spare time, raising rare strains of fungi.

Beverly had an unusual romance with a Trill named Odan. She fell in love with him and was forced to twice implant him into different hosts. She made love with him in Will Riker's body, and has felt a little strange around Will ever since. (Both Trill and host share experiences.) She had a crush on an alien known as John Doe, who transfigured into an energy being.

CHAPTER 14

GATES McFADDEN

By Alex Burleson and James Van Hise

Dr. Crusher is the first regular role in a television series for actress Gates McFadden. Her character is presented with more background than most of the others as she is the mother of Wesley Crusher, and the widow of the man who died while saving Picard's life on an earlier mission.

Gates trained to be a dancer when quite young, while growing up in Cuyahoga Falls, Ohio. "I had extraordinary teachers: one was primarily a ballerina and the other had been in a circus. I grew up thinking most ballerinas knew how to ride the unicycle, tap dance and do handsprings. Consequently, I was an oddball to other dancers."

Her interest in acting was sparked by community theatre and a touring Shakespeare company. "When I was ten, my brother and I attended back-to-back Shakespeare for eight days in a musty, nearly empty theatre. There were twelve actors who played all the parts. I couldn't get over it—the same people in costumes every day, but playing new characters. It was like visiting somewhere but never wanting to leave."

She attended several notable drama schools, including New York University, and the University of Pittsburgh. She earned her Bachelor of Arts in Theatre from Brandeis University while continuing to study acting, dance and mime. Just prior to graduation she met Jack LeCoq and credits the experience with changing her life.

"I attended his first workshop in the United States. His theatrical vision and the breadth of its scope were astonishing. I left for Paris as soon as possible to continue to study acting with LeCoq at his school. we worked constantly in juxtapositions. One explored immobility in order to better understand movement. One explored silence in order to better understand sound and language. It was theatrical research involving many mediums. Just living in a foreign country where you have to speak and think in another language cracks your head open. It was both terrifying and freeing. Suddenly I was taking more risks in my acting."

RESPECTABLE CREDITS

McFadden lives in New York City where she has been involved in film and theatre both as an actress and director-choreographer. Her acting credits include leads in the New York productions of Michael Brady's "To Gillian On Her 37th Birthday," Mary Gallagher's "How To Say Goodbye," Caryl Churchill's "Cloud 9" and, in California, in the La Jolla Playhouse production of "The Matchmaker" with Linda Hunt.

Gates was the director of choreography and puppet movement for the late Jim Henson's LABYRINTH and assisted Gavin Milar in the staging of the fantasy sequences for DREAMCHILD. "Those films were my baptism by fire into the world of special effects and computerized props," Gates reveals. She also worked on THE MUPPETS TAKE MANHATTAN, which she also appears in.

Following the first season of NEXT GENERATION, Gates was inexplicably dropped from the cast and just as inexplicably returned in the third season, after her role as ship's doctor had been played for one season by Diana Muldaur. During her absence from the series, among other work Gates had a small role in THE HUNT FOR RED OCTOBER as the wife of the main character.

During the fourth season of NEXT GENERATION, Gates McFadden gave birth to a son, James Cleveland McFadden-Talbot.

WHOOPI GOLDBERG - Crown Books signing her kids book Alice

Photo: © 1993 Ortega/Ron Galella Ltd.

The mysterious Guinan serves exotic drinks and meals in Ten Forward, but her most important role seems to be that of counselor, as she is also a fount of wisdom, giving advice and support, sometimes unsolicited but always needed, to members of the Enterprise crew.

CHAPTER 15

GUINAN

By Alex Burleson

Little is known about the hostess in the Enterprise's Ten-Forward Lounge, and many believe she works very hard to maintain that "veil of mystery" to keep herself from revealing too much to the wrong person at the wrong time. Little is known about her race and much of what is known is based solely on her report of the exact details—and she is very stingy with details.

This much is known. Guinan has a very involved history with Jean-Luc Picard. He has described it as "Beyond family or friendship" and so has she. Guinan's people are very long lived. She is believed to be approximately 700 years old. She has mentioned her father being at least that age and was alive in the same appearance in 19th century California.

Guinan had been sent by her father to visit Terra and listen to the great thinkers of the day. Guinan was able to avoid the racial persecution of the day by living in cosmopolitan San Francisco. She entertained many writers and other great thinkers of the period. She literally got a first hand education from legendary wordsmiths such as Samuel Clemens, author of TOM SAWYER and HUCKLEBERRY FINN.

When Guinan meets Clemens, her life changes in several remarkable areas. Unbeknownst to Guinan, events in the future would soon affect her present. And events in her present would affect the past and future. She would find herself in that predicament many times over the next six centuries.

IT ALL BEGAN. . .

It all began with an afternoon social tea. She had placed an advertisement that drew an unlikely party guest.

In the 24th century, a group of Starfleet archeologists uncovered a mining tunnel which had been closed since the 19th century. A pocket-watch with the initials "S.L.C.," a Colt revolver and a pair of bi-focals. And one other thing. The disconnected head of Starfleet Commander Data, Second Officer of the USS Enterprise—the only sentient android in Starfleet. A micro-organism draws the Enterprise to Davidia II, where alien predators are returning to Earth's past and stealing the life force of dying plague victims to feed their compatriots back in the 24th century.

The Enterprise discovers the temporal gateway when Data is accidentally drawn back to 19th century San Francisco, where the aliens were preying on victims of a plague. Data wins a poker game and stakes enough cash to work on his inventions. A casual glance at a newspaper used to wrap a baked item led Data to a familiar looking person.

Madam Guinan had baited Samuel Clemens into a fiery denunciation of the "Back to Earth" movement of that era. When a disturbance caught her attention. A pale-skinned man had barged in past the doorman and was disturbing the party. This was serious. There were African Queens and French Marshals in attendance. Not to mention the press. So she was ready to have him bounced out on his ear. But an inner instinct told her to listen to his story. That instinct would play a large part in the continuation of this space-time continuum.

The strange Mr. Data tells her they served on a ship together.

"A clipper ship?" she suggests.

"No, a starship," Data replies.

THINGS BEGIN TO MAKE SENCE

Clemens did not miss the inference. She realizes now this is not only a social faux pas, it could blow her cover as "a little green man." She hustles Data out of the room, convinced her father sent him and she forcefully tells him she is not through listening yet. He explains that he is an android; an artificial life form. That intrigues Guinan. She had never met an android before, and this android wouldn't meet her for 500 years, when she would know him but he would not know her.

That is when she realized how hard it would be to have advance knowledge of the future, and why it must be protected above

all her gifts. He explains how he was inadvertently drawn back while investigating the aliens intentions. Guinan is pleased to see Data instantly take her into his confidence. He must really trust the "me of the future."

Unfortunately there is a drawback. Samuel Clemens has overheard Data mention that he knew her "long lived species" had visited Earth long ago. Data had initially assumed that the future Guinan had come back to find him, but when he realizes his error he asks Guinan to help him anyway. But the man who wrote under the pseudonym Mark Twain heard every word. "The deed is done."

They continually denied any knowledge of what he was talking about, but Twain was a clever fellow. The author of A CONNECTICUT YANKEE IN KING ARTHUR'S COURT was undoubtedly intrigued by the notion of time travel. Clemens follows Data around and pesters Guinan until she finally asks him to leave. He did overhear them talk about the mine shaft they needed to find to fulfill their destiny. At Mrs. Carmichael's Boarding House, he was discovered hiding in a closet, after temporarily disabling Data's machine to track time shifts.

When the machine does detect the next shift, Data locates the rest of the Away Team from the future and rescues them in an escape from police at the Charity Hospital. They had tracked down the alien parasites and taken the snake-like entity that opened the time portal.

CHANGED FOREVER

Data brought a man to see Guinan who would change her life forever. She knew that the moment he entered the room.

She asked him, "Do you know me?"

He replied, "Very well."

She then ventured, "Do I know you?"

He smiled and replied, "Not yet, but you will." That one moment in San Francisco changed her life forever. She accompanied Picard, Data and the others to the tunnel on the Presidio military base, where she had persuaded someone to give her permission to enter. Clemens had heard of events at the hospital and high-tailed it to the Presidio where he used the Colt. 45 to take custody of the Away Team. Guinan noticed how much Clemens must mean to Picard. That meant Clemens fame would endure or Picard would be well-read, or both.

Then history exploded. The aliens appeared and attempted to take back the cane that controlled the time portal. They easily snatched it from the friendly one who called herself Troi. Guinan had felt a strange feeling when she first met Deanna. Deanna was destined to be one of the most important people Guinan would ever meet. She didn't know why, but she knew it was true.

The alien activated the device, but Data snatched it and refused to release it, allowing a resonance wave to build up and ground Data into the electrical field. His positronic circuits shut down a mere nanosecond before the head was ripped from the body in an enormous explosion.

Picard, Clemens and Guinan were knocked over, but Guinan hit her head and was the most seriously injured. The portal opened, but the entity Data was in contact with at the time of the explosion was mortally injured. The rest of the Away Team returned to the far-off world, a half millennium in Guinan's future. Except for Picard.

She was injured and he couldn't leave her to die. He knew how much she meant to him. He could not let her die or he would not live himself, and history would veer off the space-time continuum. As he cared for her he told her of what they mean to each other and how the tables will be turned in the future, when it will be her who has foreknowledge of the event instead of he.

IT WAS MEANT TO BE

Clemens did his bit to alter history by diving through the time portal and becoming the first Terran to leave the solar system. He arrived in 24th century Davidia II, but history will not record the event for five centuries. Guinan is saddened by the sight of the deactivated android head, but Picard knew that it was history fulfilling itself. She would have never met Picard if Picard didn't find Data's head in that cave five hundred years later. Picard even managed to get information to the Enterprise in the future by tapping a code into Data's positronic memory net. The code saves the entire space-time continuum when Data is reactivated seconds before the Enterprise prepares to fire torpedoes which would splinter the time-line.

Guinan, of course, knew none of this, but she had sensed things were going to turn out all right. She was beginning to realize that would become a lifelong series of things she knew that overrode logic and emotion, whether she wanted them or not. Clemens returned and Picard was able to return to the future. She told him she would see him in five hundred years. He told her he would see her in a few minutes.

After Picard left, Clemens brought medical care for Guinan and settled with Mrs. Carmichael's Boarding House. Guinan glanced at the non-seeing eyes of her automata friend and tried to get a feeling of if she would see him again. She felt she would. It wouldn't be for five centuries until she found out how close it really was.

TOTAL DESTRUCTION

Guinan suffered her greatest tragedy when she found out her homeworld had been destroyed by the

Borg. The race of Cyborg killers decimated the planet, scattering the few survivors around the galaxy. Guinan had returned to her homeworld after her stay on Earth. Some say she worked as an actress and comedienne in the late 20th century. When she arrived back home she was bonded in a "sisterhood" ceremony with a female friend of her named Delcara. Delcara had come from a planet that had been destroyed by the Borg. When the Borg killed her second family, after they killed the first, Delcara went mad and plotted revenge above all other things.

She ventured to the edge of the Milky Way and returned in a Carbon Neutronium Planet Eater which was invented by the same race of Preservers who invented the Doomsday Machine, once encountered by the original Enterprise. They were prototype weapons for combat with the Borg. Delcara used her powers of psychic projection to appear as an apparition to a young Starfleet cadet named Jean-Luc Picard in the early 24th century. He faced her again as a Captain. Picard saw Delcara die at the hands of a monstrous combination of Ferengi and Borg, using the Phaser.

Picard was beamed back to the Enterprise in a miraculous Warp 9.9 Transport, but Delcara's spirit, which lived on despite her destroyed shell of a body, was caught in an infinite time-loop. Guinan described it as like being everywhere at all times but nowhere at one. She is one of the few people capable of understanding what her "bond sister" is going through. She later encounters a malevolent entity with near omnipotent powers.

He calls himself Q and torments others which antagonize her like few beings ever have. It would be centuries before she would meet him, and unlike the Away Team, he would have memories of his dealings with her since he was at that point on the same time line, even though

for all she knew he was capable of being on several alternate time lines. She is an old nemesis of Q, however, who obviously fears her. She undoubtedly possesses powers that have never been revealed.

Her encounter with Q, two centuries ago, is another mystery, deepened by Q's revelation that she wore a different form at that time. Supposedly, her relationship with Q has something to do with her presence on the Enterprise, but, as usual, revelations about the character only deepen the mystery which surrounds her.

SON IN TROUBLE

The next time Guinan saw Q, it was two centuries later in Ten Forward. He still smarted from her besting him, but her ways always allowed her to hold Q at bay. Then Q sent the Enterprise off to meet the Borg, forever altering her world yet again.

Guinan had children over the centuries, but one would never listen. Picard said that all children had that problem. Guinan told him not in a race of listeners. The son is reported to be involved in trouble near Bajoran space and Guinan has a feeling she will have to go to Deep Space Nine to rendezvous.

When Guinan finally meets Picard in the 24th century, she has to hold back all she knows about him. While he is thinking how amazing this woman is to be attracted to him, he has no idea she has been looking at a mental image of his face for five hundred years. Later, Guinan gets into serious trouble and could even find her life forfeit. Picard intervenes and gets her out of trouble. This completely solidifies their bond and she and he interact for the rest of each other's natural lives.

He invites her to serve on the Enterprise as hostess in the new Ten-Forward lounge. She agrees and proves vital to saving the quadrant on more than one occasion. Guinan senses the arrival of Q and the approach of the Borg, but her warnings cannot head off the confrontation.

When the Enterprise-C crossed a temporal vortex and appeared 22 years later, the space-time continuum was given one of the most massive shocks ever recorded. That ship played a key role in the Federation/Klingon alliance, and without the sacrifice of that ship, the peace treaty would never have been signed.

As soon as Guinan found herself in the officers mess of a warship, with no children and surrounded by unrelenting despair, she instantly knew what had happened. In fact, she had seen it coming before it happened and steeled herself to remember what she could not. She had been watching a Klingon laugh. She had just seen Deanna Troi. They no longer existed—Tasha Yar did. Guinan could remember seeing her for years but knew they were destined to never meet. She told Picard of her feelings and he went so far as to ask the brave captain of the Enterprise-C to return to a certain death based solely on Guinan's intuition, as the alternate Beverly put it.

WRONG PLACE, WRONG TIME

Picard sends the ship back and Tasha Yar volunteers to go back with the older ship to serve as tactical officer. Captain Garret is killed during a Klingon attack in the alternate future. Guinan reveals to Tasha that she was in the wrong time-line but that Tasha would protect the outpost and save the treaty—but at a price. She would be forced to bear a Romulan's child, but Guinan would not come to know of this until years later, then they

encountered the Romulan named Sela. She did have a feeling, though.

The attempt was successful. Time shifted around her and she asked Geordi to tell her about Tasha Yar. When Sela did appear two years later on a Romulan warbird, she immediately got Picard to understand the Ramifications.

In a strange turn of events, Guinan finds herself strangely moved by her contact with Hugh, the youthful Borg whom Geordi is able to communicate with. Guinan even found that she had a deep prejudice, and although she can never forgive the genocidal race, she can forgive the individual. In fact Hugh becomes the only individual Borg in the universe. That gave her the idea that Hugh might change the race, one micro-circuit at a time. Guinan had to keep quiet during the mission to the past but did invite Picard down to tell him he had to go. If he didn't they she would die and the time-line would unravel. It was not just there, though. It was Quadrillions of beings whose existence was at stake.

When Picard entered she smiled sweetly at him. Five hundred years had passed since the moment she saw Picard leave the time-stream. Now he was walking in the door. He had said those words only minutes before by his chronometer. A half-millennium for her. As he touched her hand, the warmth of their friendship flourished.

She recently had an unusual experience in which she was altered by a Transporter and wound up inside the body of a 12-year-old child. She was thrilled. It had been centuries since she had lost her youth. And best of all it allowed her to open up to her friend, Ro Laren. Ro had a troubled past and avoided commitment. Guinan refused to listen to her prattle and became an instant friend. When Ro got into trouble with Picard, only Guinan could get Picard to listen. That act saved hundreds of lives. Guinan used to feel lonely, knowing her full empathic power and preconceptions can alter the time-stream. Now that she has finally caught up with herself, she can finally talk about it. That was the best therapy in the universe for the best therapist in the universe.

Guinan has an Imzadi of her own. His name is Jean-Luc.

Still, to most crew members who encounter her, Guinan is the 24th Century equivalent of the classic bartender, who not only serves up just the right variety of Synthehol, but also lends a caring ear and freely gives a touch of humane wisdom wherever and whenever it is called for.

CHAPTER 16

WHOOPI GOLDBERG

By Alex Burleson

Whoopi Goldberg describes her character Guinan as "a cross between Yoda and William F. Buckley," but freely admits that she's put a lot of herself into the role as well. Growing up in New York, young Whoopi was inspired by the harmonious message of the original STAR TREK, and especially by Nichelle Nichols.

When Goldberg learned that her friend LeVar Burton would be on a new STAR TREK series, she asked him to tell Gene Roddenberry that she wanted to be on the program, too—but the producers of THE NEXT GENERATION thought he was joking. A year later, Goldberg took matters into her own hands and contacted Gene Roddenberry; the two worked together to create the mysterious alien bartender who runs Ten Forward, a popular gathering place for the crew of the Enterprise.

Although Whoopi's first showbiz experience took place at the age of eight, there was a large gap in her career, as she raised a child and, at one time, contended with a heroin problem. She worked at a variety of jobs, including one in a funeral parlor whose owner had a curious sense of humor, and 'initiated' his employees by hiding in a body bin and playing "zombie," scaring them witless in the process. Whoopi was not amused.

ON TRACK

By the time the 1980's rolled around, however, she was active in theatre and comedy, working in Southern California with the San Diego Repertory Theatre and putting on a number of one-woman shows. (She also washed dishes at the Big Kitchen restaurant, where the menu still carries a special named after her.)

In 1985 she got her big break, in Steven Spielberg's film of THE COLOR PURPLE, in a role which earned her an Oscar nomination and the Golden Globe Award. Since then she has starred in JUMPIN' JACK FLASH, BURGLAR, FATAL BEAUTY, CLARA'S HEART, THE TELEPHONE, HOMER AND EDDIE, THE PLAYER and SARAFINA!

Her role as psychic Oda Mae in GHOST netted her the Oscar for Best Supporting Actress, and she continues to work in such films as THE LONG WALK HOME (with Sissy Spacek), SOAPDISH and most recently her hit film SISTER ACT, which has made over $100 million and will soon spawn a sequel. She also now hosts her own half-hour talk show, but it is not faring well in the ratings. She's had a wide variety of guests on the show, including Leonard Nimoy.

Whoopi has also won an Emmy for her 1986 guest appearance on MOONLIGHTING, and starred in the CBS sitcom BAGDAD CAFE with Jean Stapleton.

She is concerned with the plight of our nation's homeless, and has, with Robin Williams and Billy Crystal, been a prime force behind the annual COMIC RELIEF benefit concerts. In 1989, her various charity projects resulted in her being granted the Starlight Foundation's Humanitarian of the Year.

ALWAYS A STAGE PRESENCE

Still active on stage, Goldberg has performed in "Moms," "The Spook Show," and "Living On The Edge of Chaos," as well as returning to the San Diego Repertory Theatre, a.k.a. The Rep, to take part in fund raising performances (along with Patrick Stewart) for that organization. She was also one of the speakers at President Clinton's inauguration.

Goldberg continues to reveal new aspects of Guinan as THE NEXT GENERATION continues its voyages, but, as always, each new revelation only raises more questions than it answers—and that's the way Whoopi Goldberg likes it. Reportedly she is slated to make appearances in both DEEP SPACE NINE and in whatever form STAR TREK VII takes.

TRANSPORTER CHIEF

COLM MEANEY—At the world premiere of the film HERO in Century City on September 21, 1992.

A relative newcomer aboard the Enterprise, Miles O'Brien has grown from a background character into a very recognizable supporting character in the STAR TREK universe.

CHAPTER 17

TRANSPORTER CHIEF MILES O'BRIEN

by Kay Doty

According to a legend, originated and perpetuated by his father, Miles Edward O'Brien was asking for a toolbox less than an hour after making his entry into the world.

Now it is entirely true that the elder O'Brien was prone to exaggerate a bit about his son's mastery over anything with moving parts, but it is accurate to say that the boy displayed his mechanical talents at an extremely early age.

The third of five siblings born in Drogheda, Ireland near the Irish sea coast. Miles began dismantling household appliances and anything else within his reach at the age of two. By the time he was three he could reassemble most of them.

Public school was a trial for both the restless Miles, his teachers, and his parents until he was old enough to enroll in mechanical education. Delighted at the prospect of studying a subject he loved, the boy soon disillusioned when he discovered the class was composed of simple basics. Fortunately an enlightened instructor recognized the genius in the young man and transferred him to advanced engineering classes.

During his boyhood, Miles was a happy child, always ready with a joke and quick to laugh. He loved games, was popular, but in one respect he was different. He ignored the scorn of his less studious friends to spend uncounted hours studying ships, their designs, and their operation specs on vid-screens.

He never actually saw a Starship, but there was never any doubt in his mind that some day he would serve on one.

BORED NO MORE

Happy as he was with the new arrangement, Miles soon realized that to become an engineer, he would also need classes in mathematics, art and chemistry. In these he excelled proving that his earlier problems were a result of boredom.

By the age of thirteen his classmates were five to seven years his senior, but they weren't his superiors in knowledge. The final project for the term was to build, completely unaided, an operable device. Miles spent weeks closeted in the home lab he'd built in the corner of his mother's gardening shed. He secretly built, to scale, a half-sized transporter.

After successfully transporting and retrieving numerous inanimate objects, he used the family cat to determine if he could transport a living being. The experiment was successful. However, the animal did not take kindly being used as a guinea pig and was last seen running at top speed away from home and hearth.

The day arrived when the projects were to be displayed and demonstrated. While the auditorium was filling with proud parents, teachers and friends, Miles waited anxiously in the wings until his name was called. He walked on stage with his little sister's hand held firmly in his own. As previously rehearsed the little girl ran to take her place on the round disk. Before anyone realized his intent, the budding engineer stepped to the controls and a moment later the child disappeared in a sea of golden particles.

For perhaps ten seconds the stunned audience was graveyard still before Pandemonium filled the room. People gasped and leaped to their feet. His normally calm mother was screaming something about her baby, his stoic father had turned ghostly white, people were shouting and several fainted. At least one engineering instructor developed an acute case of apoplexy.

Startled by the unexpected reaction, and forgetting that she could just as easily walk back onto the stage, Miles quickly reversed the controls. Seconds later the proud little girl appeared on the disk, stepped to center stage, and smiling broadly, bowed to the stunned gathering.

CHANGING THE RULES

There was talk of expelling Miles, but a quick study of the rules revealed that he hadn't broken any regulations. In the history of the school no one had ever attempted such an ambitious project. The rules were immediately changed to cover that oversight. The teenager earned a perfect score on his project, but several Irish nervous systems would never be quite the same again.

Upon graduation from public school, Miles enrolled in Starfleet's Science and Engineering Academy. He graduated fourth in his class, applied for, and was given, an assignment in deep space.

His first ship was a small passenger liner, an assignment that gave him ample opportunity to hone his transporter skills. He didn't however get as deep into space as he would have liked. That came several years later when he transferred to the USS Rutledge under the command of Captain Benjamin Maxwell.

O'Brien was a likable, jovial man with a quick wit and ready smile. But it was his talent at repairing any malfunction that brought him to Maxwell's attention. The captain observed the young technician for several months before promoting him to the post of Bridge Tactical Officer, with the rank of Lieutenant j.g.

While serving on the Rutledge, the ship was ordered to Selik 3 where an outpost was under attack by Cardassian marauders. O'Brien was a member of the party sent into defend the residents, but the Rutledge had arrived too late. Over a hundred people at the outpost, including Captain Maxwell's wife and children, had been murdered.

A DEADLY EXPERIENCE

During hand-to-hand combat with two of the raiders, O'Brien stunned one and killed the other. He had never previously been forced to kill another sentient being and was profoundly shaken.

O'Brien was left with a deep-seated resentment of all Cardassians.

Soon after the Selik 3 incident, O'Brien earned the rank of full lieutenant and transferred to the USS Enterprise under the command of Captain Jean Luc Picard.

Lt. O'Brien served at various posts including bridge conn officer and transporter technician, and occasionally filling in as a security officer. A couple of years after O'Brien joined the Enterprise, Geordi LaForge, who had been responsible for overseeing the transporter operation, became the chief engineer with the rank of Lt. Commander. He immediately recommended that O'Brien become the new transporter chief.

The arrangement worked well, for not only was the new transporter chief one of the most knowledgeable in Starfleet, but his congenial personality made his a favorite of officers and crew alike.

VIVA LAS VEGAS

O'Brien had two passions—his love of women and gambling, not necessarily in that order. Soon after joining the Enterprise, word of his skill with a deck of cards earned him an invitation to join the officer's weekly poker game.

If O'Brien had visions of cleaning out his fellow officers credit accounts (and he did), his plans received a jolt in the person of the ship's first officer, Commander William Riker. Riker and O'Brien were both shrewd masters of the game and equally adept at bluffing. There were times when their fellow players threw in their cards and watched while the two went head to head. By the end of the first session in which O'Brien participated, no one, including Riker, considered him a patsy.

As the man most responsible for transporting people on and off of the ship.

O'Brien was seldom part of an away team. His duties included the maintenance and operation of the ship's transporter systems—to have them ready for use at a moment's notice, and to be damned certain he didn't put anyone down inside a solid wall.

Therefore he was pleasantly surprised when Commander Riker included him in an away team that would be beaming to Alphard V—the best known gambling planet in the galaxy.

HUMAN BATE

To date eighteen men, including Starfleet Captain Dale Robbins, had disappeared from Alphard V without a trace. No ransom demands issued, no bodies found, no prisoner exchange ultimatum—nothing. They were just gone.

Dressed in the latest civilian attire of wealthy tourists, O'Brien, Riker, Counselor Troi, and Lt. Worf, along with two female security guards, were bait for the kidnappers.

For a time it was a pleasant mission, O'Brien could gamble as much as he chose, in fact was ordered to do so while using Federation credits—and a very pretty security guard was to be his companion.

After the passage of three hours it became apparent that O'Brien had been selected as the next victim. This was where the kidnappers made their biggest mistake. Their ship's transporter was not functioning properly and they had inadvertently brought aboard the one man most qualified to use the problem to his advantage.

O'Brien and his companion, Ensign Jardenaux had materialized near the overhead and been unceremoniously dumped to the deck several feet below. In the scuffle that followed, O'Brien managed to activate his communicator and summon the other members of the away team to the alien ship.

In the ensuing battle O'Brien not only saved Jardenaux's life, but was able to direct the away team to the abductors' location and help recover the victims and subdue their captors.

GOOD CHOICES

Commander Riker recommended a commendation be placed in O'Brien's permanent file. But the transporter chief had one question—"Why me?"

"Because," Riker said with a grin, "of all the people on this ship you are the one I thought would be most convincing as a dedicated gambler, and least likely to be spotted as a plant."

One of his most chilling moments occurred when he risked his life to rescue Riker, Data and Troi from one of the moons of Mab-Bu VI. Riker was injured and sent to sickbay, but the other three were possessed by alien entities who had been imprisoned on the moon. The aliens planned to use the three bodies to commandeer the ship and liberate themselves from their moon prison.

The trio escaped through the desperate actions of Picard, who convinced the aliens they must return his officer's bodies and minds to their rightful owners.

THE FAMILY MAN

On the opposite end of the pleasure scale was O'Brien's marriage to Keiko Ishikawa, the ship's botanist. With Geordi as his best man, Data filling in as the father of the bride, and Captain Picard officiating, the pretty Japanese/Irish ceremony was held in the specially decorated Ten Forward. The couple later became the parents of a daughter, Molly.

After serving 22 years aboard a variety of ships, O'Brien was again promoted, and accepted a transfer to Deep Space Nine as Chief Operations Officer. Keiko and their three year old daughter accompanied him.

Upon arriving at the space station, O'Brien found that it had been trashed by the Cardassians when they were forced to leave. This meant that all the electronics on the station had to be checked out and repaired, but O'Brien proved he was up to the demands of his job.

CHAPTER 18

COLM MEANEY

by Kay Doty

When Colm Meaney's agent suggested he audition for STAR TREK—THE NEXT GENERATION, the actor not only had never seen any of the original series episodes or movies, but he wasn't even a science fiction fan.

He read for several of the main roles, and while others were chosen for those, the powers-that-be liked Meaney well enough to find occasional spots to use him.

Meaney was born and raised in Dublin, Ireland. After finishing public school he applied for admittance to the National Irish Theatre drama school. While waiting to be accepted he worked on a fishing boat. The day he was accepted at the school he gave up the professional fishing business forever.

A versatile actor who is seldom out of work, Meaney has portrayed a wide variety of roles on stage, big screen and television. He first came to the United States in 1978 and spent the next four years dividing his time between roles in London and New York before settling permanently in his adopted country. The next three or four years found him working in off-Broadway and regional theatre. His decision to move to Los Angeles in the mid 1980's brought a change to film and television.

Because of his accent, Meaney was frequently cast as a villain, but admits he likes the nice guy roles. As Chief O'Brien he has become a household name, at least among Star Trek fans, but despite appearing in nearly sixty episodes, he has not been type cast and continues to appear in other roles.

A FULL TIME PART

When Colm Meany first came in to try out for STAR TREK—THE NEXT GENERATION, the producers were looking for someone to portray the role of Data; obviously Meany was passed over for this, but he was eventually cast in the part of a nameless Transporter technician in such early episodes as "Encounter At Farpoint" and "The Naked Now."

Meaney began his STAR TREK—THE NEXT GENERATION career as a bridge officer in the first three episodes of the series. Believing that he wouldn't be used again in the series, he returned to New York to do a play, "Breaking the Code," with Derek Jacobi. When "Code" closed a year later, the writer's strike was in progress and the series was in limbo. He accepted a short-lived role on the daytime soap, "One Life To Live," that lasted until the fall of 1988 and the end of the strike.

But when the strike ended, Meany was called back by Paramount to reprise his role as the character who, after four or five episodes, was given the name O'Brien. Beginning with the strike-shortened 1988/89 season, Meaney's character was given a regular job on the ship and appeared in a personal high of seventeen episodes. The character was given the name O'Brien. Chief O'Brien, that is. His character's title was Transporter Chief. This evolved to Chief O'Brien, and in the fourth season episode "Family" he was given the full name Miles Edward O'Brien.

THERE BUT NOT THERE

The actor, who describes himself as an "irregular regular" has not appeared in as many episodes as viewers might believe. Frequently orders from the bridge to "Energize, Mr. O'Brien," continue the illusion that the actor is indeed in the episode.

But unlike Lt. Kyle, his counterpart on the old Enterprise, Chief O'Brien has been featured prominently in several episodes.

One of these was the second season "Unnatural Selection" in which O'Brien was instrumental in reversing Dr. Pulaski's (Diana Muldaur) rapid aging by skillful use of the transporter. He was also featured in season four's "The Wounded," when O'Brien talks his former captain, turned renegade, into surrendering. Meaney even gets to sing a bit in this one.

A talented comic, Meaney enjoys adding a sense of humor to his character whenever possible.

ONE MEAN MEANEY

The Irish actor has slowly been insinuating his presence into a number of movies in recent years: his big-screen appearances have included a part in Warren Beatty's DICK TRACY, his role as Dennis Quaid's brother in the Alan Parker film COME SEE THE PARADISE, the part of an airline captain in DIE HARD II: DIE HARDER, and as one of Tommy Lee Jones' henchmen in the Steven Seagal action thriller UNDER SIEGE.

Meaney demonstrated his well developed ability at playing the villain in "power Play" during the fifth season. In that episode he, Counselor Troi, and Data

were possessed by criminals long held on the prison moon Mab-Bu VI. The trio were excellent as they terrorized the ship's crew, while Meaney gave a chilling performance when he menaced his own wife and child.

The theme was again fear in "Realm of Fear" during the sixth season when O'Brien assisted Lieutenant Barkley to overcome his fear of the transporter, while explaining how he had conquered his own aversion to spiders.

Perhaps Meaney is best remembered by Star Trek viewers when, in his role of O'Brien, he became the first regular Enterprise crew member to be married on screen. His beautiful bride, Keiko, was played by Rosalind Chao.

Fans have frequently asked about the similarities between Meaney and James Doohan (Scotty in the original series) and their Star Trek roles. Both O'Brien and Doohan's Scotty are in engineering, and both characters are very good at their jobs, but there the similarities end.

Doohan was, and is, well known for his ability to portray a variety of accents, while Meaney's accent is his own. Meaney hails from Ireland and Doohan was born in Canada. One thing the actors do have in common—both are well received guests at conventions.

JUMPING SHIP

As his presence on the series became more frequent, Colm Meany's character began to take on a more prominent role, emerging as an important supporting character. When Rick Berman and Michael Piller began casting DEEP SPACE NINE, then fourth Star Trek series (counting the short-lived animated series), Meaney decided to jump ship and become a regular on the new show—a promotion for both Meaney and his alter-ego, O'Brien. So now Meany has moved on to the more crucial leading role as the chief engineer on the ramshackle space station, Deep Space Nine.

Meaney is married and has a pre-teenaged daughter, Brenda, who is an ardent fan of STAR TREK.

Space does not permit a complete listing of all of Meaney's work, however in addition to those mentioned above, his credits include THE GAMBLER III, MOONLIGHTING, COME SEE THE PARADISE, REMINGTON STEELE, FAR AND AWAY, TALES FROM THE DARK SIDE, PERFECT WITNESS and dozens of others.

SECURITY CHIEF

DENISE CROSBY - At the play "Brooklyn Laundry",
Coronet Theatre.   Photo: © 1993 Ortega/Ron Galella Ltd.

The legendary Tasha Yar, she who died in the line of duty, only to live again in a world which was never meant to be. . . so that she might once again make the ultimate sacrifice for her shipmates.

TASHA YAR
SECURITY CHIEF (FIRST SEASON)

By James Van Hise & Laura Schoeffel

Tasha grew up on a failed Earth colony where law and order had broken down and the survival of the fittest became the order of the day. When she was five her parents were killed in a gang fight, leaving Tasha alone to take care of her sister, Ishara. Tasha blamed the gangs for the death of her parents and refused to join them. This left Tasha on her own to protect herself from the rape gangs and drug lords of her home world, Turkana IV.

An orphan, she spent her nights and days foraging for food and fleeing the roving rape gangs. The colony broke down due to being comprised largely of renegades and other violent undesirables who were being given a second chance. A sample of what life was like there was briefly seen in "The Naked Now", while later developments were seen in the episode entitled "Legacy."

In her teens, Tasha escaped to Earth, leaving behind her sister, Ishara, who remained by choice. Ishara eventually joined one of the gangs and thought her sister was a coward for leaving her homeworld and joining Starfleet. Ishara's opinion of Tasha changed when she met her sister's crewmates. She worshipped the order and discipline of Starfleet because it is the exact opposite of the chaos she grew up fighting.

Captain Picard requested that Tasha be his chief of security on the Enterprise when he witnessed Tasha cross a minefield to rescue a comrade. At 28 Tasha was one of the younger members of the bridge crew and often had feelings of not being good enough to belong with the rest of the Enterprise team.

NOT WORTHY

From her perspective, the Enterprise command officers were something akin to saints. In her eyes they were better than her because she grew up in such a terrible environment. She eventually became close to all her fellow officers on the Enterprise but felt a special fondness for Lt. Worf, Wes Crusher and Commander Riker.

Tasha viewed Wes Crusher as the ideal boy, growing up in a warm, loving environment with plenty of friends. Tasha and Worf shared a fondness for combat. Worf thought it was a sure thing that Tasha would win the ship's martial arts competition and had been helping her train for it before she was killed. Commander Riker made Tasha laugh, something she had not been able to do very much when she was growing up. She viewed Captain Picard as a father figure and was constantly trying to impress him.

She was one of the few crew members who performed the same duties on and off the ship. When an Away Team was selected to investigate a landing site, whether for a possible shore leave or for a conference that Captain Picard is being called to attend, Yar, as Security Chief, was always a part of the initial contact team.

Captain Picard, having visited Tasha's homeworld, her "hell planet," understood what she went through and became her mentor. He taught her to apply the cushioning of history and philosophy to her almost obsessive need to protect the vessel and crew.

A SEXY MIX

Tasha was of Ukrainian descent. This, combined with her own strict exercise regimen, gave her a quality of conditioned, subtle beauty that would have flabbergasted males from earlier centuries. With fire in her eyes and a muscularly well-toned and very female body, she was capable of pinning most crewmen. She was also an exciting sensual and intellectual challenge to men who enjoyed full equality between the genders. Neither Number One or Picard was blind to these qualities.

The episode "Hide And Q" suggested that she was attracted to Picard but because he was the captain, was not willing to be involved with him. The episodes "Skin of Evil" and "Where None Have Gone Before" also suggested that she and Geordi might have had some kind of relationship. In her holographic farewell, she tells Geordi that he helped her see the positive side of things and she also paused before speaking to him, suggesting that she was trying to think of something to say to such a close friend.

In "The Naked Now," Tasha revealed a previously concealed interest in Data. She even went so far as to take him into her quarters and seduce him! When the judgment-inhibiting effects wore off, Tasha realized that she had completely violated her personal sense of decorum, and told the literal minded android that "It never happened." Since she didn't specify what "it" was, Data was a bit confused as to what, exactly, had never occurred. Tasha was at first embarrassed by the incident, but later came to accept it without bitterness or pain.

Tasha's death at the hands of the creature Armus was a senseless tragedy which left her comrades stunned and bereaved. Oddly enough, it seems to be the emotionless Data who cherishes her memory the most; he keeps a holographic snapshot of her among his most cherished possessions.

The Enterprise crew later encountered Ishara Yar, Tasha's sister, when they went to rescue a Federation freighter's crew from captivity on Tasha's hellish home world. She reminded them of Tasha, but she was using them to get help for her political faction. Perhaps she was as capable of loyalty and friendship as Tasha, but Ishara's loyalties were bound up in the ongoing struggle of her world, and she lacked the courage to turn her back on the chaos and follow her sister's path.

DEAD AGAIN

In "Yesterday's Enterprise," due to a bizarre rip in the time stream, Tasha lived to alter history. In the alternate time stream the Federation was at war with the Klingons. When Guinan informed this Tasha that she had died a meaningless death in an alternate time line, Tasha asked to go back in time on the Enterprise 1701-C.

The Enterprise C had been helping a Klingon Outpost that was under attack by the Romulans, and it was hoped that this action would help to avoid a long war between the Federation and the Klingons. The Enterprise C was destroyed but its mission was successful, as war did not break out between the Federation and the Klingon Empire after all. As it turned out, the doom, while certain, was somewhat delayed.

In the fourth season cliffhanger "Redemption I," we see a Romulan commander who looks exactly like Tasha Yar. In "Redemption II" we learn that the woman's name is Sela and Tasha Yar was her mother. Tasha Yar had been captured by the Romulans due to the events set in motion in "Yesterday's Enterprise" and became a Romulan general's consort in order to save the lives of other crewmembers who survived.

Tasha and the Romulan had a daughter, Sela, who became a Romulan commander. When Sela was four years old, Tasha attempted to escape from the Romulan home world. According to Sela, Tasha was discovered trying to escape and was executed by the Romulans. Sela does not miss her mother and believes that Tasha deserved her fate.

CHAPTER 20

DENISE CROSBY

by Laura Schoeffel

The granddaughter of Bing Crosby, Denise was born and raised in Hollywood, California. "My grandfather was a Hollywood legend. Growing up with that wasn't exactly normal or typical either, and I think that helps me understand Tasha's imbalance and insecurities," explained the actress in a first season interview.

Soon after graduating from Hollywood High School, Denise took time off to travel to South America and later began a brief modeling career in Europe where she was a runway model for designers like Yves St. Laurent. Prior to getting involved in developing an acting career, Denise went through what she describes as her "European runway model thing. I hated modeling, but I was taken to Europe by three California designers who were trying to launch their fashions there. I loved London, so I just stayed on."

She later posed for photos in Playboy magazine which caught the eye of casting director Toni Howard. Upon returning to the United States, Ms. Howard contacted Denise about the possibility of an acting career and had her audition for a role in the film DIARY OF A TEENAGE HITCHHIKER. While Denise didn't get the role, she enrolled in acting classes and got an agent.

Denise made her film debut in 48 HOURS and also had roles in the films TRAIL OF THE PINK PANTHER, CURSE OF THE PINK PANTHER, DESERT HEARTS, THE MAN WHO LOVED WOMEN, ELIMINATORS and MIRACLE MILE. Her television credits include DAYS OF OUR LIVES and L.A. LAW. Denise has also appeared in LA stage productions of "Tamarra" and "Stops Along the Way."

A rock and roll fan, Denise has also appeared in music videos with Mick Jagger, the Tom Tom Club, and Chris Isaak. Her big break was landing the role of Tasha Yar in STAR TREK—THE NEXT GENERATION.

LOOKING FOR SATISFACTION

Denise Crosby described the character she played with this thumbnail sketch. "She comes from an incredibly violent and aggressive Earth colony where life was a constant battle for survival. She can fight and she knows her job, but she has no family, is emotionally insecure and somehow feels that she doesn't quite belong on this ship of seemingly perfect people."

Ironically Denise had originally auditioned for the role of Counselor Troi and Marina Sirtis was auditioning for Tasha Yar. After three readings the producers switched the actresses. As the first season progressed, Denise became dissatisfied with the way the character of Tasha was being handled. "Too many episodes went by where I was just merely floating around in the background or kind of assisting someone in some way. And for me, as an actor, it was really dissatisfying. And it's a very difficult show with nine characters at that point, to make it work."

She approached the writers with ideas for stories involving Tasha, but when nothing came of those ideas she eventually took her concerns to Gene Roddenberry. "Why I was killed off was really Gene's idea because the character was not going to go very far, he felt. He couldn't give me a definite answer as to where Tasha was going in the next season. Would I get better scripts or have more to do in the show? Would I be more involved in stories in different ways? She he didn't want me to go but he left that decision for me."

Making the decision was not easy and not a decision Denise made by herself. She talked with the other cast members about it and even approached the writers with ideas about the character. "I came up with ideas, the writers came up with ideas, the producers loved them all, said great let's do them, and nothing ever happened. So then I decided that the only thing to do really was for me to move on. It was great to do the first year, but better to make a statement on a strong note than to just fizzle out after six years of being on a show.

OUT IN A BLAZE OF GLORY

When it was decided that I would leave the show, Gene really felt that the strongest way to go would be to have me killed. That would be so shocking and dramatic that he wanted to go with that. Unfortunately with STAR TREK it's very hard to keep anything secret. Before you knew it we were getting reports—I hear one of the regulars is going to be killed. It wasn't such a big surprise. I think in retrospect, perhaps Tasha should've really gone out in a blaze of glory. There's never any real battles ever fought. The show is never supposed to be about violence and it shouldn't be. But I think if you have one

cause for there to be a show about a real violent battle, that was it. Let's see this supposed expert security officer do her stuff."

After leaving THE NEXT GENERATION, Denise went on to make several movies including PET SEMETARY, SKIN DEEP, DOLLY DEAREST, HIGH STRUNG, TENNESSEE WALTZ, ARIZONA HEAT and THE RHYTHM OF SILENCE. She has also guest starred in several television shows including THE FLASH, HUNTER, DARK JUSTICE, JACK'S PLACE, MANCUSO F.B.I. and appeared a music video with Dolly Parton. More recently, Denise appeared in one of the segments of the Showtime anthology RED SHOE DIARIES.

Denise has also appeared in some local Los Angeles theatre productions, including the critically well-received "Tamara", in which she had the lead, as well as the controversial one-act play "Stops Along The Way" directed by Richard Dreyfuss.

Denise returned to THE NEXT GENERATION as Tasha Yar in the third season episode "Yesterday's Enterprise." This led to her playing the part of Tasha's daughter on THE NEXT GENERATION. "The part of Sela sort of came about from me sitting around in my house one day thinking about how much fun it was for me to go back and do 'Yesterday's Enterprise,' and it was so much fun that I thought what else can I do? I thought it was pretty well established that Lt. Yar and Lt. Castillo on 'Yesterday's Enterprise' had something going and so perhaps they had a child or Yar was pregnant when she went back into the past to fight her final battle. And I sort of thought it out and it seemed to really make sense, and there were no flaws.

"So my original intention was that Lt. Yar would have a daughter that was raised by the Romulans and would grow up to try to actually be a Romulan. So I brought this up and the producers really liked the idea and they sort of toyed with it for a while. A few months went by and I got a call and they said we like your idea but we just can't make sense of that Lt. Yar got pregnant by Castillo. We'll have it so that Yar was captured, they didn't all die in the battle, the ship was captured and she was taken by a Romulan general." Since then the character of Sela has also appeared in the two-part episode "Unification" with special guest star Leonard Nimoy.

Denise is currently one of the stars of the Fox Network series KEY WEST. Denise plays a character named Chaucy Caldwell, who she describes as "a Southern, right wing aristocrat who is very different than anything I've done. She's sort of very old money and very right wing and Republican and an alcoholic. It will give me a chance to do comedy, which I really have wanted to do. Most people have seen me in really serious roles or I get cast as the real strong, determined, able to handle herself, modern woman. So this gives me the chance to fall apart in front of your eyes."

RO LAREN

A Bajoran, Ro Laren is the most recent addition to the crew of the Enterprise, although her ultimate role in Starfleet and the STAR TREK universe has yet to be truly defined and may have been more short-lived than most fans would have wished.

CHAPTER 21

RO LAREN

The fiery Bajoran freedom-fighter joined Starfleet in an effort to help her people, but things went terribly wrong. The time Ro was young cannot properly be called a childhood. She grew up in a refugee camp, watching her family and friends die from the Cardassian ethnic cleansing. The Cardassian occupying army, under Gul Dukat, took her father away from the camp.

When Ro was seven years old, a Cardassian officer gave her sugar candy, then she watched her father beg for his life as he was slowly tortured to death. The humiliation made her hate her own race, her own self, until she learned to fight back. Ro attended Starfleet Academy, was quickly promoted to Lieutenant (j.g.) and was on her way to a bright future in Starfleet, bringing great pride to her people. At least that was the plan.

Life went tragically wrong for Ro when the young officer disobeyed a direct order and eight of the members of USS Wellington's Away Team were killed as a result of her insubordination. Laren offered no defense of her actions on Garon II, so she was summarily court marshaled and packed off to prison. She was assigned to the stockade at Jaros II. She is stunned to learn that Admiral Kennelly wants to use her to help Bajoran terrorists in exchange for weapons and other items. Ro agrees to help her people.

When Ensign Ro Laren is transferred to the Enterprise, it is at the command of Admiral Kennelly, who is using her to help him accomplish a secret aim he has worked out with the Cardassians that Ro knows nothing about. Picard is angry at the transfer as it was made without consulting him. Riker dislikes the idea as well. They mistrust her, but Kennelly states that because she's Bajoran, her experience will help them locate Orta, a terrorist who has supposedly been attacking both Cardassian and Federation outposts.

THE FEELING IS MUTUAL

Ro reports for duty she makes it clear that she doesn't like the assignment either, but it's better than prison, which is where she had been languishing until Kennelly freed her. She wants the assignment completed as quickly as Picard does. Her advice is immediately helpful as she teaches Picard the protocol of Bajoran names (last names first), and in who to talk to about intelligence.

The Enterprise visits Valo Three to meet with Jas Holza at a Bajoran refugee camp. They hope to find a lead to Orta. But Ro isn't impressed with Holza and explains that he's just a figurehead used to deal with the Federation by the Bajorans, but he has no real authority. Ro recommends they go to meet with Keeve Falor. When Ro and Picard meet with Keeve

Falor, he states that he won't help the Federation because in the past they used the Prime Directive as an excuse to allow the Cardassians to repress the Bajorans. Picard is troubled by the conditions he sees in the camps and orders blankets and medical supplies for the people there. After that Keeve agrees to help Picard, with some prodding by Ro Laren.

Guinan decides it's time to meet and get to know this mysterious and aloof Ensign Ro. She approaches Ro in Ten Forward, but Ro states that she wants to be left alone. Ro is clearly unhappy and embittered, but Guinan is unflappable and presses Ro for more conversation. Guinan wants to know about what really happened on Garon Two, but Ro doesn't care to discuss it. People died, Ro was guilty. What more need be said.

In spite of Ro Laren's expressed annoyance with Guinan, she sees something in Ro that she likes. Ro leaves when she is notified that a subspace message has come in for her. Ro takes it in her quarters. It's from Admiral Kennelly and it's clear that she is on a private mission for the Admiral which Picard knows nothing about.

ON HER OWN

The Enterprise arrives at the third moon of Valo One where they are scheduled to meet soon with Orta. Ro chooses to go on ahead without telling anyone and beams down six hours ahead of schedule. Riker is furious when he discovers this. The rest of the Away Team beams down to search for her and Orta. but no sooner do they appear in the caverns inside the moon than they are surrounded by Bajoran terrorists and taken prisoner.

Orta meets with Picard but states that he mistrusts the Federation. Orta denies any involvement in the attack on the Federation colony. He points out that their ships only have impulse power and are not capable of standing up to Federation starship technology. Could someone else be trying to draw the Federation into the Bajoran conflict?

Back aboard the Enterprise, Picard makes it clear that he is furious with Ro Laren and restricts her to quarters for not following protocol. Guinan visits Ro and convinces her to talk to Picard. Guinan brings Ro to Picard where she confesses that Admiral Kennelly assigned her to this mission to secretly offer arms to the Bajorans—a clear violation of Federation policy.

Ro confesses that she hates the Cardassians because when she was seven she was forced to watch them torture her father to death. Picard accepts Ro's admissions and asks her to convince Orta to go along with a plan which could expose the conspiracy. The Enterprise contacts Admiral Kennelly and informs him that they've made a deal with Orta and will escort Orta's ship to a Bajoran camp on Valo Three.

DEEP SPACE TAIL

During their voyage to Valo Three, two Cardassian warships are detected following them. The Enterprise intercepts the Cardassian ships which demand that the Bajoran terrorists be turned over to them. They give the Enterprise one hour to withdraw. Picard contacts Admiral Kennelly, telling him that the Cardassians seemed to know their exact course and that Orta would be aboard the small ship. But Kennelly recommends giving up the terrorists rather than risk offending their Cardassian allies. Picard accuses the Cardassians of plotting to involve the Federation in the war, but withdraws the

Enterprise. The Cardassians move in and destroy the Bajoran ship.

Captain Picard reveals to Admiral Kennelly that he has evidence that the Cardassians staged the attack on the Federation colony on Solarian Four, then tricked Kennelly into supporting their plan to capture the Bajoran terrorists. For engaging in tactics against Federation policy, Kennelly faces a probable courts martial.

Picard invites Ensign Ro to remain in Starfleet and on the Enterprise. She is reluctant, but agrees so long as she can wear her Bajoran earring even though it's not part of Starfleet regulation uniform. She and Picard beam up from the Valo Three where they had been visiting the Bajoran refugee camp.

When the Enterprise encounters a disaster in deep space and is crippled, with many parts of the vessel sealed off, Ro finds herself in conflict with Counselor Troi, who is with her on the bridge and is the highest ranking officer there in the crisis. Picard and Riker and cut off from the bridge elsewhere in the ship.

When massive systems failures sweep the ship, emergency bulkheads close, sealing off the decks, trapping people in various parts of the ship. The engines are off-line and life support is operating on backup systems.

The Enterprise has hit a quantum filament. When a second one hits the vessel, Monroe is killed on the bridge at her computer console when it explodes. Troi and O'Brien remain on the bridge and they cannot raise Picard on the communicator.

On the bridge, O'Brien transmits a distress call but can't be sure it's going out. Ensign Ro makes it to the bridge by climbing up the turbolift shaft, but they're trapped there. With Monroe dead, Troi finds herself the senior officer on the bridge. Ro and O'Brien discover that the matter-anti-matter containment field is weakening. If it drops to 15% the ship will explode.

STANDING FIRM

Ro Laren suggests a saucer separation to get away from the drive section. Troi instead instructs them to divert power to engineering to enable anyone there to see the danger and prevent the containment breach. Ro protests, stating that they have no evidence that anyone is even there. Ro keeps pressing to have a saucer separation or risk having everyone die. Only if someone in engineering notices the readings and acts can the ship be saved in time.

In Engineering, Data's head is attached to the computer. Riker notices the containment field readings and following Data's instructions, helps Data to stabilize the containment field in the matter-anti-matter chamber. On the bridge they see this and realize that someone was in engineering, and that now the ship is saved. Ro does not apologize for her suggestions as she was doing only what she believed was right, just as Deanna Troi was in refusing to buckle under to Ro's demands.

On Stardate 45494.2, the Enterprise encounters a conundrum when it is investigating subspace signals in the epsilon solar system which may indicate intelligent life there. Ensign Ro is having another argument with Commander Riker about her arbitrary changes of procedure without seeking permission first.

Just then the Enterprise encounters a small vessel which begins scanning them. Suddenly the computers go down and a wave of light sweeps through the inside of the ship. When it passes, no one can remember who they are or what they're doing there.

They detect debris nearby, which leads them to believe that they may have been attacked. They try to interface the computer but cannot call up anything other than the directory. Worf asks the crew throughout the ship to report on their status. They determine that the Enterprise has one thousand people on board, all without memories of who they are. Because of the weaponry the ship carries, they believe that they must be on a battleship. Worf points out that they should first make certain that they are battle ready.

WHO'S WHO?

Commander Riker and Ensign Ro, their differences wiped away along with the memories of their identities, check out the ship together. They are very friendly towards one another even though they don't know who they are. In Ten Forward they find Data working as a bartender, not that they know whether he's supposed to be there or not.

When they finally access identity records, Worf discovers that he's the security chief and feels chagrined. The computer records indicate that the Federation is at war with the Lysians and that their mission is to attack Lysian Central Command.

Troi questions whether the information they have is valid since they have no way of double-checking it. But Picard points out that their orders insist that they maintain radio silence. Troi says that nothing feels right, but she seems attracted to Riker. And she's not the only one. When Riker returns to his quarters after getting off duty he finds Ro Laren there and likes the idea. She comes on to him and he responds.

The Enterprise enters Lysian space where they encounter and Lysian

destroyer. Picard resists attacking it even though MacDuff thinks they should. When the Enterprise refuses to reply to its hailing, it attacks. Picard fights back, destroying it. The Enterprise continues on its mission.

Troi tells Riker that she doesn't feel right about the war. Geordi is suspicious because anything in the files relating to personal knowledge is missing.

Picard remains suspicious of the situation, as though he's being set up. MacDuff agrees but says they could be prolonging the war by not following orders.

A MONSTER WITHIN

The Enterprise nears the Lysian Central Command. They find little armament or firepower as they destroy unmanned sentry pods. They reach the Central Command and sensors reveal that fifteen thousand people are on the station.

Riker wonders how their mortal enemy could be one hundred years behind them in weapons technology. MacDuff insists that they attack. He tries to take command and when Worf resists, he attacks Worf. Worf and Riker fire hand phasers, which reveal MacDuff to be a non-human who is stunned unconscious.

The Enterprise leaves Lysian space and is bound for Starbase 301. The crew's memories have been restored. The impostor is a Satarran, a race long at war with the Lysians. The Satarran's needed the Enterprise technology to fight the Lysians.

When Riker once again encounters Ro and Troi in Ten Forward, he finds that the two women are amused by what happened, and particularly at Riker's embarrassment over his enthusiastic role in the menage. But Ro does not express any regrets. She seems to be fitting into the Enterprise crew even better than she thought possible.

Ro Laren is also on hand when alien entities take over the bodies of Data, Troi and O'Brien in a blatant power play to free their fellow entities who remain marooned on the surface of an M Class moon of Mabu Six.

The three interlopers enter Ten Forward and commandeer it. When Worf and a security team arrive, they shoot it out with Troi, Data and O'Brien. But Worf and the team are stunned while Troi, Data and O'Brien seem strangely immune to the phasers.

Riker dispatches security teams to cover the entrances to Ten Forward while O'Brien takes the Transporters off line. Picard contacts Ten Forward to discuss terms. Data threatens Worf who refuses to show fear. Amid those in Ten Forward who are among the cowering hostages is Keiko, O'Brien's wife, with their baby daughter.

Picard offers to trade himself for the wounded hostages and the impostors agree. After Picard enters Ten Forward, he meets with Troi, who seems to be the Trio's leader. She claims to be Bryce Shumar of the starship Essex. She says that the other two are her officers from the Essex. She says that all she wants is to get her crew's remains from the planet where their consciousness have been trapped for two hundred years.

Geordi and Ro Laren set up a microscopic drill above Ten Forward. They plan to shock the entities out of Troi, Data and Ro and then trap them in a containment field. When the plasma field is activated it only snares Troi and O'Brien. Data goes wild, grabbing Picard by the throat and stating that he'll kill everyone if they're not released. Picard orders the attack to stop and the entities return to the bodies of Troi and O'Brien.

The three each take a hostage and go to the cargo bay. Once there Picard

challenges Troi/Shumar to reveal who they really are as he can't believe that Federation officers would act so dangerously.

On the bridge, Riker explains that Picard directed them to that cargo hold because it's possible to blow the outer door which would send everyone in the hold out into space. He tells Ro Laren that he'll blow the hold when he thinks there's no other choice.

The other entities are beamed up from the planet, whereupon Troi reveals that they are all actually condemned prisoners sentenced to that moon five hundred years before. When a containment field is thrown around the new entities, Troi threatens to kill everyone, but Picard replies that they're all willing to die to save the ship from them. Picard offers to return them all to the surface if they free them. Troi reluctantly agrees. She warns Picard not to pass this way again. The entities free the bodies of Troi, Data and O'Brien and the prisoners are transported back down to the surface of the cold and lonely moon.

Ensign Ro finds herself a prisoner of a time loop, along with the rest of the Enterprise and its crew when they encounter a mysterious cause and effect in space.

ENTERING THE UNKNOWN

It is Stardate 45652.1 and the Enterprise enters an area of space called the Typhon Expanse. They're the first Starfleet vessel to chart this unexplored region. When they finally escape the time loop, thanks to Data and Riker, they discover that the Enterprise was in the time loop for seventeen days. The other vessel which emerged from the space distortion just in front of them, and which caused the strange occurrence, is the USS Bozeman, a Federation ship, Soyuz Class, a type not used for eighty years.

Ensign Ro's strangest experience occurred along with Geordi and involved a strange experiment gone awry on a disabled Romulan ship.

When the Enterprise is on its way to lend assistance to a Romulan ship in distress, Geordi, Riker and Ro Laren are assigned to beam over to the Romulan vessel. Ro thinks it's a mistake to help them. They beam over and find a lot of damage from some sort of explosion. The Romulan's replicators are off line so Geordi and Ro beam back to the Enterprise with the graviton generator to repair it—but there's a problem during transporting and they vanish en route. Councilor Troi cannot detect any sign of them and their patterns cannot be located. Geordi and Ensign Ro are declared dead.

Picard orders the Transporters shut down and shuttles used to go back and forth to the Romulan ship. The Enterprise moves off some distance as the Romulan ship is still in danger of exploding. The engine core has to be ejected from the Romulan ship and the Enterprise extends their shields to protect the other ship when the core explodes in space.

Aboard the Enterprise, Capt. Picard walks right by Ro without seeing her. She's lying on a corridor floor and wakes up. She enters Sickbay but no one pays any attention to her. Ro overhears Picard and Dr. Crusher talking about her but no one can see or hear her. In fact, Capt. Picard walks right through her as though she's an invisible ghost. Ro attempts to communicate with Dr. Crusher, but to no avail.

On the Romulan ship, power is transferred from the Enterprise so that the other ship can make it back to Romulus.

TO BE OR NOT TO BE

Geordi encounters Ro Laren and has already discovered the same things that she has. They discover that they are solid to each other. Ro believes that they're spirits or souls—that they've died. But Geordi dismisses that as a possibility.

Data investigates the accident and detects Kromiton particles from the Romulan ship's cloaking device. Data decides to investigate further aboard the Romulan ship.

Ensign Ro has gone to the Enterprise bridge to say good-bye to what had been her life. She believes herself dead and that she is experiencing what it is like to be a ghost. Picard and Riker enter the bridge and she hears Riker say that he wants to speak at Ro's memorial service. Ro is very curious over what he plans to say.

Geordi finds Ro and tells her that they have to go with Data on the shuttle to the Romulan ship. Geordi convinces Ro that if he's right then he'll need her help, and if he's wrong then it won't matter anyway. Ro reluctantly agrees to accompany him. She still thinks that they're both dead.

On the Romulan ship, Geordi and Ro look around with Data investigates. Geordi finds a strange phase invertor which could have been combined with a cloaking device. But they have to find a way to be de-phased.

The Romulans are concerned about their interphase generator being discovered so they plan a way to sabotage the Enterprise. Geordi and Ro overhear. But unknown to them there is a Romulan present who has also been phased and he follows them.

Geordi and Ro return to the Enterprise on the shuttle, but the Romulan follows as well. Data detects more

Kroniton fields on the Enterprise. Geordi realizes that he and Ro are leaving the Kroniton fields whenever they touch something.

Ro encounters the Romulan who points a disruptor at her and wants to know where Geordi it. The Romulan wants to know how to be de-phased and thinks they may have the answer.

Geordi is trying to alert Data to his presence and guesses a way he might be brought back.

The Romulan leads Ro at gun point but she attacks him and flees. The Romulan follows, firing his disruptor. Data tracks the new Kroniton fields this unleashes. The Romulan catches up to Ro and they get into a hand-to-hand fight. Just then Geordi comes upon them and rams into the Romulan, knocking him through the bulkhead into space.

The new engine core is installed in the Romulan ship and the Enterprise prepares to leave. Geordi and Ro want to get to where the Kroniton decontamination is and see if it will make them briefly visible. They go to Ten Forward where there will be sure to be a lot of people. They arrive in Ten Forward to find a real party going on as people share their memories of Geordi and Ro.

Ro sets her disruptor to overload and its explosion dramatically increases the Kroniton fields. The decontamination field is increased as well, causing Geordi and Ro to partially materialize. Picard and Data witness this and the android figures out what to do.

Geordi and Ro reappear, much to everyone's surprise. Geordi tells Capt. Picard about the Romulan sabotage to the Enterprise.

Ro and Geordi, alone, have their first meal in two days. Geordi is digging in but Ro seems distracted. She admits that for awhile she thought she was dead and had begun to believe in what the Bajorans

had taught about the afterlife, but now she doesn't know what to believe.

Geordi says they should develop their own interphase device because if it can teach Ro Laren humility, then it can do anything. Ro finds the observation amusing.

Although Ro Laren has remained with the Enterprise, she has been little seen of late, except when a Transporter malfunction transformed her back into a child. Picard has said that she would have made Lieutenant Commander if not for the incident on Garon II.

Ro has a great deal of sympathy for Picard, particularly after the brutal torture he received at the hands of the Cardassians when they lured him into a trap. Ro may occasionally return to Bajora and probably will have to travel through Deep Space Nine to get there.

CHAPTER 22

MICHELLE FORBES

Actress Michelle Forbes began as a dancer along with her sister. Michelle wasn't as interested in the world of dance as her sister was, and in fact realized that acting was what she really wanted to pursue when she saw her mother performing on the stage. She proved her seriousness by attending the Performing Arts High School in Houston, Texas and began doing stage work there.

While on a two week vacation in New York City she auditioned for a film and shortly thereafter signed with the William Morris Agency and then relocated to New York to pursue professional acting full time. Her first major role was a three year stint on the soap opera GUIDING LIGHT where she played twins.

She learned a lot about the ins and outs of professional acting and her exposure on GUIDING LIGHT enabled the actress to land guest-star roles a several prime time television series. Her last role prior to appearing on THE NEXT GENERATION was on the short-lived, but critically acclaimed, series SHANNEN'S DEAL.

Ensign Ro was not the first character she played on STAR TREK. She'd previously had a guest-star role as the character Dora in "Half A Life." When she auditioned for that episode she read with David Ogden Stiers, since she was to play his daughter. Stiers, of course, played the central character, Dr. Timicin, in that story which dealt with a world where people are expected to commit suicide when they reach the age of sixty so as not to become a burden on their family or society. Her biggest scene in "Half A Life" occurs when Dora comes on board the Enterprise to beg her father to reconsider his plan to leave home and not commit ritual suicide. Dora clearly hated Lwaxana Troi for her influence on her father. This brief scene caught the eye of the production team.

STATUS QUO

When the actress returned to THE NEXT GENERATION, At age 26, Michelle Forbes found herself stepping into the full blown character of Ensign Ro, essentially starring in the episode which bore her character's name. But in spite of the immediate popularity of the character, she was only committed to appear in a few episodes in the fifth season, and has appeared in only one in year six.

Forbes seemed to like this status, though as it allowed her the opportunities to pursue other roles while still being connected to an on-going series. But unlike the series regulars she isn't tied to the series week in and week out. At the time she was initially involved with THE NEXT GENERATION she stated, "Because of my excellent experience with the cast and crew so far, I would not at all hesitate to sign a long-term contract and become a regular cast member of this series. Having a steady job is always pleasant. No matter what happens, I don't see myself getting type-cast in this role."

The actress describes Ensign Ro as being very tough and very shut down, but when she went to prison she finally came to terms with herself and her heritage, but she is by no means at peace with herself. "She is very tortured and has a difficult time dealing with people. Ensign Ro is an excellent role to play."

At the time, Forbes hoped that the writers would explore her character's past a lot more as a great deal was hinted at but left unresolved in the debut episode of Ensign Ro. For instance, while she is a bit abrasive with some crew members, particularly Riker, she has become friendly with others, most notably Geordi LaForge and Guinan. But the real harsh secrets of her past have not been delved into. "Nobody really knows what her troubles were or where her dark side comes from. I'm sort of enjoying playing a character with such a mysterious past. I don't want to see her get too soft. I like the severity of her personality."

JAGGED EDGE

This edge her personality has is what many fans welcomed about her character. While everyone else aboard the Enterprise seems to be the best of friends, with never a harsh word to pass their lips, Ensign Ro is the only recurring character who is allowed to be cranky and get into arguments with anyone. But by having her aboard the humanity of all of the characters is magnified by showing that there's more beneath the surface than the more than one hundred episodes aired ever even hinted at.

Playing an alien requires that Michelle Forbes have special make-up applied to her nose. Although this looks like a minor touch when we see it in the show, the make-up session done to accomplish this lasts two hours, although that would include the normal makeup every actor wears in front of the camera as well.

While the character of Ensign Ro was well received, Michelle Forbes apparently backed away from her initial interest in appearing in a series regularly as she was offered the chance to continue playing Ensign Ro as one of the major characters on DEEP SPACE NINE, but she turned it down. The role was then rewritten so that while the character on DEEP SPACE NINE is still a Bajoran, it is no longer Ensign Ro, who's future is largely shrouded in just as much mystery as her past.

Meanwhile, Michelle Forbes has gone on to motion picture roles, including a co-starring part in KALIFORNIA in which she appears with Juliette Lewis and Brad Pitt. Michelle also stars with Adam Ant in THE RELUCTANT VAMPIRE. Although Forbes has shied away from signing on as a full-time cast member on either THE NEXT GENERATION or DEEP SPACE NINE, she will continue to make guest appearances on both TREKs. She was interviewed by NEW VOYAGES about her commitment to TREK.

"The production values on the show are incredible, and it's really nice to know that if something is going to be around and if you're committing yourself to celluloid history, it's STAR TREK. Right now, out of all the shows on television, this is probably the only one that's going to be around in ten years that people are going to know and watch. I don't think they'll be watching CIVIL WARS, so it's nice to know there's a great team behind you that's going to make it look good and write well for it.

"I love everyone who works on the show," Forbes continues. "The stories are very interesting. It's a wonderful place where imagination runs wild and that's rare and a lot of fun. On all levels, in writing, acting, sets—it's a wonderful place to be and be around."

STAR FLEET OFFICER

WIL WHEATON - Headshot at the Creation Convention.
Photo: © 1993 Ortega/Ron Galella Ltd.

He has exited the series—twice (both gracefully and ungracefully) but may yet reappear from time to time. While he was along for the ride, his voyage was a controversial one.

CHAPTER 23

WESLEY CRUSHER

By Alex Burleson

The son of Jack and Beverly Crusher, Wesley has inherited the genius of both of his parents. This is apparent in his superior memory and his insight into the mechanics of computer circuitry and starship warp engines. He not only sees how the different parts of a mechanism work together (and sometimes why they don't), but he also senses the alternative ways that the same components can be joined to produce alternative results. This was evident in the incident chronicled in "The Naked Now" when he was able to use the tractor beam as a deflector beam and buy the Enterprise crucial time it needed to warp out of orbit.

It is important to understand that Wesley's abilities are not merely limited to the ability to visualize the starship's design and functioning. A computer could accomplish as much. What Wesley can do in addition is to visualize the potential of these designs and circuitries in almost unlimited combinations. In "Where No One Has Gone Before," Wesley befriended the alien who calls himself The Traveler and recognized that the being was manipulating the starship's warp drive in unique ways. The Traveler later confided to Captain Picard that Wesley is one of those rare individuals possessed of a gifted insight into the understanding of how the universe works. This is a secret that Captain Picard has not shared with Wes, his mother nor with anyone else in order to allow the boy to develop normally.

In recognition for the important assistance Wesley provided in "Where No One Has Gone Before," Picard has appointed Wes an acting Ensign with full access to the bridge. He has also tendered the boy's application to the Starfleet Academy. Previously Picard had ordered that no children be allowed on the bridge and had even become aggressively annoyed when, after allowing Wesley to sit in the center seat, the boy responded to an instrument warning instead of letting Picard do so.

Wesley's father was Jack Crusher, a Starfleet officer, was killed while serving under Captain Picard on the USS Stargazer. Although the boy may not be aware of it, he possesses many of the strengths and qualities that made his father a valuable Starfleet officer. Picard recognizes this and feels that it is his duty to his old friend to encourage those strengths to bloom into their fullness.

CRUSHER(ING) MOMENTS

Wesley was slated to be executed by the Odo of Rubicon III, before Picard talked the "gods" of the Edo out of the execution.

When Wes fell in love with a princess, destined to rule a world, he was shocked to discover that she is an isomorph (a non-human shape-shifter).

On a mission, Picard and Wesley are aboard the mining shuttle Minivik when it crashes on the moon, Landa Paz, in orbit around Pentaurus III, Picard is injured trying to save Wes's life. Wes repays Picard, by nursing the injured captain through the ordeal.

Wesley is the "father" of the sentient species of living computer chips, called Nannites. He was in the middle of an experiment with them when two escaped and soon took over entire regions of the ship's computer. When Wes returned on leave, to the Enterprise, he arrived just in time to stop a plot to use mind-control games to subvert the Federation.

Wesley's new love interest is Mission Specialist Robin Leffler. She helps him overcome the plot, before she herself is overcome by the "Game." Wes's most serious problem to date came following an accident around Titan, largest moon of Saturn. Wes' Nova Squadron is destroyed during a collision and all but one, Joshua Albert, survive.

Josh was a friend of Wes and he had trouble going along with the well-meaning cover-up, which Picard, Data and Geordi figure out. Picard confronts Wes, bringing up his history on the ship. Picard reacts to Wes much as Boothby did to Picard in a similar situation in Picard's Academy days. Wes finally stands up and admits to the cover-up. He is held back a year and placed on probation. His squadron leader takes responsibility for the incident and is expelled.

[In a future history, predicted in Peter David's novel IMZADI, Wes grows up to become Captain Wesley Crusher of the USS Hood. Married twice, father of three.]

CHAPTER 24

WIL WHEATON

By Alex Burleson

California born, Wil's first professional work was a TV commercial when he was seven for Jell-O pudding pops opposite Bill Cosby. A Few years later, Wheaton appeared in a Los Angeles theatrical production of Arthur Miller's play, "All My Sons" in 1980.

His first serious acting role on television was opposite Timothy Hutton in A LONG WAY HOME, an NBC movie made for television in 1981. This was followed by a CBS Schoolbreak Special, THE SHOOTING.

The young actor's first feature film appearance was opposite Richard Dreyfuss and Susan Sarandon in THE BUDDY SYSTEM. Wil also had guest-starring roles in three TV pilots, A LONG TIME GONE, 13 13th AVENUE and THE MAN WHO FELL TO EARTH. Wil also had a featured role in the television remake of THE DEFIANT ONES, which starred Robert Urich and Carl Weathers. He had roles in the films HAMBONE AND HILLIE (with screen legend Lillian Gish) and THE LAST STARFIGHTER and also did one of the character voices in the animated film THE SECRET OF HIMH (he was the fat rat named Martin).

His other television credits include appearances on FAMILY TIES, ST. ELSEWHERE and HIGHWAY TO HEAVEN as well as the TV movie YOUNG HARRY HOUDINI. One of his post-TNG appearances was the cable TV movie THE LAST PROSTITUTE. His most recent role was in the 1993 HBO cable movie A DEADLY SECRET which dealt with the subject of teen suicide.

THE BREAKTHROUGH

Wil Wheaton came to true Hollywood prominence as 12-year old Gordie Lachance in STAND BY ME where he achieved great reviews as one of the boys in Rob Reiner's hit adaptation of Stephen King's novella "The Body." This was followed up by his portrayal of the world's most famous stage magician in the NBC television movie YOUNG HARRY HOUDINI.

In 1987, Wil Wheaton starred in the low-budget film THE CURSE, which was a very loose adaptation of the H.P. Lovecraft story "The Color Out Of Space." This film also featured a role for his sister Amy, who was ten years old at the time.

Wil was the youngest "old Star Trek fan" when he joined the cast of THE NEXT GENERATION at age fifteen. When his agent called him about auditioning for the new series, he said, "Sounds great!" He thought it sounded even greater when he landed the role.

Wheaton was excited to be part of the new adventure and had soon dubbed his fellow cast members with appropriate (or perhaps inappropriate) nicknames. Dudley DoRiker was soon bestowed upon Jonathan Frakes; for Michael Dorn, Wheaton devised "Turtlehead," "Zippy the Android" for Brent Spiner, and "Pookie" for Denise Crosby. Patrick Stewart was nicknamed Old Baldy, but this was not Wheaton's idea but rather that of Stewart himself (perhaps a pre-emptive strike on his part).

WIL'S CRYSTAL BALL

Wil Wheaton's creativity in the nickname department did not extend to the realm of prognostication. A second season interview found Wheaton making various predictions for the third season, such as the assertion that Gates McFadden would never return to the series and the statement that an operation would restore natural sight to Geordie LaForge. (Admittedly, this second notion had been bandied about but it never came to pass.)

Wil initially described his character as, "very smart. He's not your typical wise-cracking 15-year-old. He inherited the genius of his mother, and his father, a Starfleet commander." The best thing about his character is that he's not treated like a kid. "At first I thought, okay, but I hope it isn't, kid gets in trouble, crew gets kid out of trouble. But it's not like that at all. Wesley is almost an equal with the rest of the crew. He knows the Enterprise inside and out, backwards and forwards. The ship's operations manual is like his Bible, and his big goal is to get on the bridge and control the ship."

At fifteen, the young actor had a simple goal for the future. "I want to buy a beach house in Malibu and surf my life away. But you know, I'm 15 years old, and if you set your goals and dreams too far in the future, you've got to wait a long time."

Out of all the characters on THE NEXT GENERATION, Wesley was the closest to Roddenberry's heart as the character was named after himself, Wesley being Roddenberry's middle name. He even considered Wes to be sort of an idealized version of himself, which is why Roddenberry was annoyed when the character quickly came under a lot of criticism.

NOT TOO LIKEABLE

In the first season, Wesley saved the Enterprise more than once and this seemed to be the extent of his character. But in the first season episode "Justice," Wes did get in trouble and did have to be saved by Picard, in spite of the actor's description of his character to the contrary.

But the biggest problem with Wes in the early episodes is that he was profoundly annoying. He had an ever present idiot grin on his face and seemed to be much younger than his years. The fact of the matter is that children are already getting older faster even in the 20th century. That a fifteen year old in the 24th century would act like an arrested twelve year old was just poor writing. This was straightened out eventually but not until the actor was old enough to outgrow the willingness to act in this manner.

As for Gates McFadden, Wheaton was rather disappointed at her departure after the first season, as they only had a few scenes together in which to explore their familial relationship. Fortunately, her return for the third and subsequent seasons resolved this problem.

Wheaton himself was not unaware of some negative audience reaction to his character, but he took it all in stride. It bothered him but he just got on with his life rather than allowing it to get to him. Admittedly, the use his character was put to early in the series—saving the ship at every turn as it if were an extra-credit project for some science class—was a bit annoying. Even Wheaton himself was annoyed by this and lobbied for better use of the character.

The controversy regarding Wesley Crusher was all over the pages of the fan magazines and at the 1987 Loscon in Los Angeles, a panel was held specifically to discuss the "Wesley Problem." What made it even more interesting was that Wil Wheaton was in the audience and agreed to participate in the panel, and tried to defend the portrayal of his character. After all, at that time the series was barely two months old.

A few months later Gene Roddenberry was confronted with some of the same questions at the Museum of Broadcasting in Los Angeles. Roddenberry seemed taken aback and explained that it was just coincidence that those scripts which were approved by that time happened to include major plots involving Wesley which sometimes included him saving the Enterprise.

Wil Wheaton was defensive on this subject for a long time as no other character on the series garnered anywhere near the criticism that his did. When he left the series as a full time regular in the fourth season, it was so the actor could attend college and do more film roles.

MATURING

He appeared in two episodes in the fifth season, including "Code of Honor" in which Wes was portrayed as being capable of perfidy. After all, even though he finally admitted to the cover-up that he and his classmates had engaged in, Wes was literally forced to admit it under threat of Picard exposing it himself and forcing Wes to call him a liar if Wes hadn't already admitted the truth.

Had Picard not privately confronted Wes over this incident, it is clear that Wes never would have admitted the truth otherwise. This was a far more interesting "final" episode for Wesley Crusher than the fourth season exit for him was. And should Wesley return in any future episode, this disgrace would color anything which happened therein.

Wil Wheaton once remarked on an incident in which William Shatner encountered the cast of THE NEXT GENERATION. "One day our cast was in the commissary and Mr. Shatner came up and it was real tense. He said he liked it. When Captain Kirk likes the next generation, it's a big deal." This may well have occurred after a more notorious encounter. During the production of STAR TREK V: THE FINAL FRONTIER, Wil Wheaton visited the set of the motion picture while Shatner was directing.

When the young actor introduced himself and revealed that he had a station on the bridge of the new TV Enterprise, Shatner reportedly expressed amazement and ridiculed the notion of a child on the bridge, reportedly upsetting Wil Wheaton. A person who was working on the film at the time stated that Roddenberry complained to Harve Bennett (the producer of the second through the fifth STAR TREK feature films), who strongly suggested that Shatner apologize to Wheaton, which he did.

HIS SPIRIT REMAINS

Although he's been off the series for more than a year, Wil Wheaton's alter ego Wesley Crusher still remains somehow present on the STAR TREK—THE NEXT GENERATION in spirit. The character, which admittedly annoyed many fans early in the series' run was clearly being groomed for some sort of future—as part of the next NEXT GENERATION, perhaps— as early as the earliest episodes.

But even while STAR TREK fans allowed themselves to get unnecessarily vexed by the presence of a teenager on the Enterprise bridge, Wil Wheaton had more pressing concerns: he hated the "youthful" sweaters he was obliged to wear in his early outings. When Wesley was given a commission and bridge duties, some viewers may have winced but Wheaton was relieved: he could finally trade in his despised sweaters for a genuine Starfleet uniform. The character's elation was a reflection of the young actor's own feelings about the wardrobe change.

In later episodes, such as his final appearance as a regular cast member on the series, audiences saw Wheaton as a maturing Wesley Crusher. And in a guest shot in "The First Duty," viewers saw Wesley actually get in serious trouble at Starfleet and face a difficult moral decision to boot. All along, it would seem that much of the problem with Wesley lay in the writing; and older Wesley gave the series scripters more to work with. As for Wil Wheaton, there is little faulting his mature work, and one can easily imagine that there will be a place for his character in many STAR TREK epics to come.

DOCTOR

CHAPTER 25

DR. KATHERINE PULASKI/ THE ACTRESS, DIANA MULDAUR

After Doctor Crusher goes on to head Starfleet Medical, Doctor Pulaski comes aboard as her replacement. There is nothing known about Pulaski's background and at the end of the season she was gone. She was transferred off the Enterprise, apparently because she just couldn't mix that well with the crew. She had a particular problem dealing with Data, whom she could not help but regard as a machine and not a person.

For the duration of the second season of STAR TREK—THE NEXT GENERATION, the cast was joined by a new doctor, a temporary replacement for Gates McFadden's Beverly Crusher: Dr. Katherine Pulaski. But while the character, actually intended by Gene Roddenberry as a permanent replacement for Dr. Crusher, was new to the STAR TREK universe, the actress portraying her was not. Diana Muldaur appeared in two episodes of classic Trek. Oddly enough she played doctors in both outings: the blind Miranda Jones in "Is There In Truth No Beauty?" and Anne Mulhall in "Return To Tomorrow."

At the time of her landing the role of Dr. Pulaski, Muldaur and her husband had been living in the mountains for some time and had not seen the new STAR TREK series, a problem that was easily alleviated by sending her over a dozen videotaped episodes of the new Enterprise's adventures. Impressed by the fine ensemble acting of the cast, Muldaur was anxious to join in the latest leg of the Trek through the future.

However, she found the transition was not a completely easy one, observing that, "It was a very difficult thing to adapt to. But everybody was warm and wonderful. Nobody knew who I was and they were all staring at me strangely and wondering what I would do next. I think it took a couple of shows to begin feeling at home. It took a lot of adjustment. Not being able to really explore the character and just beginning with the first show was hard."

But Muldaur quickly discovered that both cast and crew of THE NEXT GENERATION were a delight to work with, calling them "probably the most professional I've ever worked with."

ONE IN THE SAME

Muldaur saw the character of Katherine Pulaski as a crusty one, "a strong person on the outside but not tough." Basically a strongly opinionated person herself, Muldaur was able to bring much of herself to Pulaski's character. "She does terrible thing," admitted Muldaur in 1989, "like interrupt people all the time. . . which I also do." Muldaur could not help but be amused when the series writers, observing this shared trait, wrote an episode in which Pulaski kept interrupting every character she talked with!

Diana Muldaur's acting career began on the stage in the Sixties with the New York-based APA theater group. She appeared on Off-Broadway in "The Balcony" (at twenty-five dollars a week!) and soon moved to Broadway, appearing in such plays as "A Very Rich Woman," "Seidman And Son," and with Donald Pleasance, in "Poor Bitos."

Muldaur's television career is a long and exemplary one. In addition to her STAR TREK work in the Sixties and the eighties, she also appeared in the Gene Roddenberry project PLANET EARTH (a sequel to Roddenberry's previous telemovie GENESIS II). Other television of note included her recurring role as Dennis Weaver's girlfriend in McCLOUD. She also appeared in THE SURVIVORS, THE TONY RANDALL SHOW and BORN FREE.

After her departure from STAR TREK—THE NEXT GENERATION, she went on to a choice role on L.A. LAW... until that character's fateful encounter with an elevator shaft. In addition to her acting career, she was also the first woman to serve as the President of the Academy of Television Arts and Sciences, after serving on the executive board of the Screen Actor's Guild.

When she is not acting, Diana Muldaur's activities include sailing, skiing, and fishing, in addition to raising Airedale Terriers. Her thirty dogs are all show champions.

A MATTER OF FIT

Her tenure on STAR TREK—THE NEXT GENERATION only lasted a single season as Gene Roddenberry reconsidered his dismissal of Gates McFadden and reinstated Dr. Beverly Crusher on board the Enterprise. Dr. Katherine Pulaski vanished from the show without the slightest explanation and, beyond one offhand reference to one of her medical innovations, she was never mentioned again.

To be perfectly honest, while Diana Muldaur, a fine actress, may have fit in well with the cast of THE NEXT GENERATION, her character never quite found her place on the show. This was no fault of Muldaur's; the character was ill-considered, Roddenberry's attempt to create a female "Bones" McCoy, as evidence by Pulaski's inexplicable hostility towards Data—an attempt to recreate the McCoy/Spock friction of the original series—and her phobia of using the Transporter, which she seemed to have inherited directly from McCoy!

In general the character, through no fault of the actress playing her, did not achieve any real chemistry with the other cast members. Diana Muldaur's work was fine, only hampered by scripts and by Roddenberry's faltering creativity; all in all, she has earned her place in the world of STAR TREK.

THE ENTERPRISE

The Enterprise NCC 1701-D is the fifth starship to bear that name. This new vessel is twice the length of the ship that Captain Kirk was familiar with 80 years before and has nearly eight times the interior area to house the crew. The basic structure is the same even though the vessel looks more sleek and cohesive.

CHAPTER 26

THE ENTERPRISE NCC 1701-D

While the first starships to bear the name Enterprise were designed to represent the Federation in matters both political and military, the 1701-D is designed for exploration, de-emphasizing the importance of being a battle cruiser. This Enterprise has been designed to be the home of 1,012 people, which is two and a half times the ship's complement of the Enterprise 1701-A. This is the result of a century of technological evolution emphasizing human interaction with the hardware they use.

This technological progress has been dubbed "Technology Unchained". What this means is that technical improvement has gone beyond developing things which are merely smaller, faster or more powerful but has become centered on improving the quality of life of the people the hardware was designed for. The reason this is of particular importance aboard the new Enterprise is that the crew consists of many families. Thus, service in Starfleet no longer means that families are separated for many long months but can stay together on this, the first Starfleet vessel of this class.

As the first captain on this bold new experiment in human exploration, Picard is uncomfortable with the idea of dealing with families. He's accustomed to a crew of professional, Starfleet-trained men and women who know their duty and understand their jobs thoroughly. The concept of children and other non-Starfleet personnel running around unnerves him even though he understands that it contributes to the morale of those hardy men and women who will be called on to labor aboard this starship for many long months. Non-crew spouses and children are rarely seen in the command and duty areas of the ship. In "The Last Outpost" Riker enters the lounge behind the bridge and encounters three young children whom he escorts out, kindly reminding them that they are not to be in that area.

The sophistication of the new Enterprise includes a variety of single and group family modules, various levels of schools, study facilities and other features designed so that children and spouses can live lives as normal as possible aboard what is practically a colony ship. recreation has always been a facet not neglected on starships but now this role has been expanded with the presence of children.

There is a large selection of entertainment, sports and other recreational forms, but the most elaborate by far is the Holodeck. The Holodeck, as seen in "Encounter At Farpoint," can simulate almost any landscape or sea world complete with winds, tides, rain or whatever is needed to make the illusion convincing to the tactile senses. They achieve an amazing sense of reality and are employed in both education and recreation, as studies of other worlds can be richly enhanced by a holographic simulation of the society or climate in question.

The Transporter beam has a range of 16,000 kilometers (roughly 10,000 miles). The Transporter is also designed to filter out viruses, bacteria and other alien matter which might be picked up on the surface of a planet. It can also be used to detect and, if necessary, de-activate weapons.

A special feature of the new Enterprise is the ability of the saucer section of the vessel to separate from the main hull in emergency situations. The only drawback to this escape procedure is that the warp engines are located in the main hull while the saucer section contains only Impulse Power from an engine located at the rear of the saucer. Earlier versions of the Enterprise also contained this feature but it was never employed in any of the stories chronicled before "Encounter At Farpoint."

There are also shuttlecraft aboard the Enterprise which are used when the Transporter is malfunctioning or should the starship become disabled and evacuation in deep space become a necessity. One must assume that there are enough shuttlecraft that hold all aboard the Enterprise, lest the tragedy of the legendary Titanic be repeated.

THE WRITERS' BIBLE

In 1987 Roddenberry wrote the writer's guide for the then aborning series STAR TREK—THE NEXT GENERATION. This was written by Roddenberry as a guide to the writers who would be setting stories aboard this new and even more amazing 24th century craft.

WHAT IS CHANGED?

"Beyond the vessel's familiar symmetry, many things. The starship is designed to be home (home in a very literal sense) to 1012 persons. Gone is the metallic sterility of the original ship, the reason being that the last century or so has seen a form of technological progress which 24th century poets call 'Technology Unchained' — which means that technical improvement has gone beyond developing things which are smaller, or faster, or more powerful, and is now very much centered on improving the quality of life."

STARSHIP INTERIORS

"The living and working areas of the Enterprise reflect this emphasis on the quality of life by a lighter, brighter and more comfortable feeling everywhere. The starship's duty areas are no longer cluttered with the same profusion of gauges, instruments and control buttons. Instead, not only the bridge but all other parts of the vessel feature black panels which on touch or voice command will become information displays. This is usually accomplished by a crewman speaking the key words, 'Show me. . . ' followed by a statement of what is desired. (Audio answers are triggered by the command, 'Tell me. . . ') The 'Show Me' command causes the requested information to come into view on the formerly black surface. If one wants to manipulate either that information or some starship mechanism, touch buttons can be displayed at the same time."

THE BRIDGE

"Because of this starship's level of automation, the new bridge looks very different from the one in the original Enterprise. Gone is the need for officers to report for work to a giant cockpit lined with rows of duty stations studded with clusters of instrumentation and controls.

"Instead, our new bridge combines the features of ship control, briefing room, information retrieval area and officers' wardroom. In other words, much the same kinds of things happen here as in the old bridge but with less emphasis on the mechanics of steering the starship. It is a place where the starship officers with either aboard or away responsibilities can meet, check out information, make plans, or just catch up with what is happening.

"Who actually drives the Enterprise? The job of starship command and control is handled by two bridge duty officers at positions known as CON (command and vessel control including helm and navigation) and OPS (vessel operations including jobs which were once engineering functions.) These jobs can be handled by the appropriate series regulars or by others when needed. All such things are handled with the same casual effectiveness as in the past—more like the exchange between civilian airliner professionals than between military persons.

"From the moment the starship's destination is selected and the journey begun, every detail of the voyage is guided and monitored by sophisticated 24th century sensor/computer combinations. 'Routine' emergencies are sensed and analyzed with counter-measures already underway long before human help is possible or even desirable."

THE BRIDGE SET

"The COMMAND AREA of our bridge is a semi-circle of control seats where the Captain and his next-in-command and advisors are located. Just ahead of this are two FORWARD STATIONS, OPS and CON positions. These stations are often manned by Data and Geordi LaForge. (Yes, the Enterprise is being driven by a blind man.)

When either Data or La Forge leave their stations, they are promptly replaced by supernumerary officers who will be referred to be the nicknames of these stations.

"The rear of the bridge has a raised semi-circular area, separated from the Command Area by a railing which is also a set of console stations. This is the TACTICAL CONSOLE. At this position, Tasha plus any necessary assistants are responsible for weaponry, defensive devices (shields, etc.) plus ship's internal security.

On the rear wall of the bridge are the Aft Consoles. These five stations are generally unsupervised functions unless specifically needed at any given time. Viewing them from left to right, they are as follows:

Emergency Manual Override: In the event of main computer failure, many of the ship's primary functions can be operated from this station.

Environment: This can adjust the Life Support systems and related environmental engineering functions anywhere on the ship. A similar system was employed against the bridge crew in Kirk's time in "Space Seed" as well as against Khan's cronies during the same encounter. No doubt this is to prevent the vessel from being used as a weapon against its inhabitants.

Propulsion Systems: This is a backup system to OPS and CON which ties in directly to Engineering and the control of the warp drive and impulse engines.

Sciences: This is essentially a research station generally unmanned except for research purposes. It is used by the Science Officer and various mission specialists and can also be accessed by the Chief Medical Officer.

Sciences II: This is a second console identical to the Science station next to it so that more than one researcher at a time can access information and interact.

"On the stage-left side of the bridge are two turbo-lifts and a door leading to the Captain's Office (sometimes called the Captain's Ready Room). On the right side of the bridge is a door leading to the bridge head and washroom."

MAIN VIEWER

"The forward part of the bridge is a large wall-sized holographic 'viewer.' This main viewer is usually on and will dominate the bridge and the action as the original framed view screen could never do."

BRIDGE LOUNGE

"Just behind the bridge is a large room filled with comfortable furniture and lined with huge windows facing rearward and giving a spectacular view of the aft top portion of the saucer section and the rest of the starship. This lounge has complete food facilities and is often used as an observation deck and retreat for bridge officers."

CAPTAIN'S OFFICE/READY ROOM

"On the left side of the bridge (facing forward) is a door leading to the Captain's Office. Also known as the Ready Room, it has an auxiliary turbo-lift and the Captain's private head and washroom.

"The Ready Room is intended as a private place for the Captain, offering both a confidential place to work and

convenient rest; but it serves a second and equally important dramatic function: it can also be used for personal and private conversations."

THE STARSHIP: A NEW LOOK

"As in the original series, the Transporter Beam is a device which allows us to instantaneously transmit crew or cargo from one location to another. The Transporter effect will be much the same as before, but with improved detail and dazzle. Also, a Transporter effect reverse angle will sometimes be used, which will be the optical effect as seen from the perspective of a person actually being beamed somewhere.

"The Transporter Room itself is no longer a metallic battleship gray. As in the original series, a person being transported from the ship must stand on the Transporter platform while the command 'energize' is given. To Transport from away, the individual uses his communicator to request 'beam me up' which allows the starship Transporter Chief to lock onto that person's position.

"Decontamination. It will be established that the Transporter is designed to filter out viruses, bacteria and other alien matter that might be picked up on an away visit. The Transporter Beam is primarily a line-of-sight device; its range is about 16,000 kilometers. (10,000 miles.)"

COMMUNICATOR

"The communicator is now worn as part of the familiar Starfleet insignia. In addition to providing communications as before, its monitoring functions remain in full operation constantly, allowing the starship command officers to monitor the safety and progress of a landing team at all times. Although this creates some additional difficulty in maneuvering our people into danger, story believability demands that our 24th century technology be at least as capable as 20th century technology in this area—perhaps not such a difficulty if one realizes that 24th century 'villains' are no doubt capable of technological countermeasures."

CHAPTER 27

THE STARSHIP: STANDING SETS
SICK BAY

"As in the original series, but vastly improved: A three room complex including Dr. Crusher's office, a set of diagnostic beds with complete medical monitoring, and a state-of-the-art medical research facility."

CORRIDORS

"Again, as seen in the original series, but without the same battleship sterility. The new corridors are wider and more friendly-looking and (as elsewhere) will include vegetation."

UTILITY CORRIDORS

"Redress of the corridors to suggest that this is the major access to the ship's behind-the-walls machinery. Like the Jefferies Tubes, the utility corridors may be lined with light-fiber cables and tubes to suggest the ship's internal nervous system and plumbing."

JEFFERIES TUBE

"A cylindrical utility tube lined with electrical conduits and light-fiber cables, the Jefferies tube is large enough for a human being to crawl through. Jefferies Tubes provide direct access to various parts of the ship's control mechanisms and computer monitoring systems."

ENGINE ROOM

"Our new Engine Room contains a huge matter/anti-blender. It is open at one end to convey a sense of greater space. The Engine Room is located near the base of the main module of the ship."

TRANSPORTER ROOM

"There are several Transporter rooms throughout the vessel. The one we will see most frequently will be an updated version of the original Transporter room and, as before, a Transporter chief stands at a separate console opposite the Transporter dais."

PERSONAL QUARTERS

"Each person on the Enterprise has personal quarters of his/her own. These quarters are much more spacious and livable than we have seen in the past. It is possible that one wall of the personal quarters may be a 'holographic window' much like the Holodecks: each person's quarters will reflect his or her own background and tastes. (This will be a standard set, redressed as necessary.)"

INT. TURBOLIFT

"The turbolifts allow our crew members to travel from any part of the Enterprise to any other; the turbolift travels both vertically and horizontally. The interior is a comfortable, relatively spacious cabin."

INT. SHUTTLECRAFT

"The Enterprise shuttlecraft is a small, but comfortable landing vehicle for travel between the ship and a planet when the Transporter is not available or practical to use. The interior of the shuttle can seat several people comfortably."

COMMUNITY AND FAMILY LIFE

"As humanity probes deeper and deeper into space with ten-year or longer missions becoming the norm, Starfleet has begun encouraging crewpersons to share the space exploration adventure with their families. Twenty-fourth century humans believe that Life should be lived, not postponed.

"Previous experiences in space exploration have underscored the lesson that people need people for mental and physical health. Starfleet encourages its people to participate in family and community life and bonding.

"Although non-crew spouses and children are rarely seen in the command and other duty areas of the vessel, the sophistication of starships now includes a variety of single and group family modules, various levels of schools and study facilities, a large selection of entertainment, sports and other recreation forms, and contests (electronic and other) of a thousand kinds."

HOLODECKS CAN SIMULATE ANY ENVIRONMENT

"The Enterprise Holodecks can duplicate with startling reality almost any landscape or sea world complete with winds, tides, precipitation, and whatever. These decks are much used in both education and recreation and are even more important in preventing crew and families from feeling that they are leading contained and limited lives. In the Holodecks, almost any kind of recreation, training or exercise can be simulated, especially since these same decks can also make potent use of the starship's gravity control system. This also permits, for example, the challenge of skiing any real or imaginable slop or engaging in an exciting variety of mid-air low gravity games and contests."

Thus we have a fairly complete view of the Enterprise 1701-D as it was originally conceived by Gene Roddenberry (and his uncredited collaborators). It's easy to see how the 23rd century model was revamped and remodeled to produce the more modernized 24th century version—which actually better reflected the strides in computer technology which the 20th century had witnessed in the Seventies and Eighties.

Cast honored by the Starlight Foundation with the "Childern's Friendship Award"
at the 10th Annual "The Child In All Of Us" Gala.

THE MAN WHO CREATED STAR TREK: GENE RODDENBERRY

James Van Hise

The complete life story of the man who created STAR TREK, reveals the man and his work.

$14.95 in stores ONLY $12.95 to Couch Potato Catalog Customers
160 Pages
ISBN # 1-55698-318-2

TWENTY-FIFTH ANNIVERSARY TREK TRIBUTE

James Van Hise

Taking a close up look at the amazing Star Trek stroy, this book traces the history of the show that has become an enduring legend. James Van Hise chronicles the series from 1966 to its cancellation in 1969, through the years when only the fans kept it alive, and on to its unprecedented revival. He offers a look at its latter-day blossoming into an animated series, a sequence of five movies (with a sixth in preparation) that has grossed over $700 million, and the offshoot "The Next Generation" TV series.

The author gives readers a tour of the memorials at the Smithsonian and the Movieland Wax Museums, lets them witness Leonard Nimoy get his star on the Hollywood Walk Of Fame in 1985, and takes them behind the scenes of the motion-picture series and TV's "The Next Generation." The concluding section examines the future of Star Trek beyond its 25th Anniversary.

$14.95.....196 Pages
ISBN # 1-55698-290-9

COUCH POTATO INC.   5715 N. Balsam Rd   Las Vegas, NV 89130   (702)658-2090

Use Your Credit Card 24 HRS — Order toll Free From: (800)444-2524 Ext 67

TREK: THE UNAUTHORIZED BEHIND-THE-SCENES STORY OF THE NEXT GENERATION

James VanHise

This book chronicles the Trek mythos as it continues on T.V. in "Star Trek: The Next Generation," telling the often fascinating conflict filled story of the behind-the-scenes struggles between Roddenberry and the creative staff. It includes a special section on "Star Trek: Deep Space Nine," a spin-off of "The Next Generation," which will begin syndication in early 1993.

$14.95.....160 Pages
ISBN 1-55698-321-2

THE NEW TREK ENCYCLOPEDIA

John Peel with Scott Nance

Everything anyone might want to know about the Star Trek series of television shows and movies is conveniently compiled into one volume in *The New Trek Encyclopedia*.

This detailed volume covers the original T.V. series, all six feature films, "Star Trek: The Next Generation," and the animated show. It provides descriptions, explanations, and important details of every alien race, monster, planet, spaceship, weapon, and technical device to appear in all the shows—all listed in alphabetical order for easy reference. It also includes every person who worked on the shows or movies!

$19.95.....300 Pages
ISBN 1-55698-350-6

COUCH POTATO INC.   5715 N. Balsam Rd   Las Vegas, NV 89130   (702)658-2090

Use Your Credit Card 24 HRS — Order toll Free From: **(800)444-2524** Ext 67

BORING, BUT NECESSARY ORDERING INFORMATION

Payment:
Use our new 800 # and pay with your credit card or send check or money order directly to our address. All payments must be made in U.S. funds and please do not send cash.

Shipping:
We offer several methods of shipment. Sometimes a book can be delayed if we are temporarily out of stock. You should note whether you prefer us to ship the book as soon as available, send you a merchandise credit good for other goodies, or send your money back immediately.

Normal Post Office: $3.75 for the first book and $1.50 for each additional book. These orders are filled as quickly as possible. Shipments normally take 5 to 10 days, but allow up to 12 weeks for delivery.

Special UPS 2 Day Blue Label Service or Priority Mail: Special service is available for desperate Couch Potatoes. These books are shipped within 24 hours of when we receive the order and normally take 2 to 3 three days to get to you. The cost is $10.00 for the first book and $4.00 each additional book .

Overnight Rush Service: $20.00 for the first book and $10.00 each additional book.

U.s. Priority Mail: $6.00 for the first book and $3.00.each additional book.

Canada And Mexico: $5.00 for the first book and $3.00 each additional book.

Foreign: $6.00 for the first book and $3.00 each additional book.

Please list alternatives when available and please state if you would like a refund or for us to backorder an item if it is not in stock.

COUCH POTATO INC.   5715 N. Balsam Rd   Las Vegas, NV 89130   (702)658-2090

Use Your Credit Card 24 HRS — Order toll Free From: **(800)444-2524** Ext 67

ORDER FORM

___ Trek Crew Book $9.95	___ Number Six: The Prisoner Book $14.95
___ Best Of Enterprise Incidents $9.95	___ Gerry Anderson: Supermarionation $17.95
___ Trek Fans Handbook $9.95	___ Addams Family Revealed $14.95
___ Trek: The Next Generation $14.95	___ Bloodsucker: Vampires At The Movies $14.95
___ The Man Who Created Star Trek: $12.95	___ Dark Shadows Tribute $14.95
___ 25th Anniversary Trek Tribute $14.95	___ Monsterland Fear Book $14.95
___ History Of Trek $14.95	___ The Films Of Elvis $14.95
___ The Man Between The Ears $14.95	___ The Woody Allen Encyclopedia $14.95
___ Trek: The Making Of The Movies $14.95	___ Paul Mccartney: 20 Years On His Own $9.95
___ Trek: The Lost Years $12.95	___ Yesterday: My Life With The Beatles $14.95
___ Trek: The Unauthorized Next Generation $14.95	___ Fab Films Of The Beatles $14.95
___ New Trek Encyclopedia $19.95	___ 40 Years At Night: The Tonight Show $14.95
___ Making A Quantum Leap $14.95	___ Exposing Northern Exposure $14.95
___ The Unofficial Tale Of Beauty And The Beast $14.95	___ The La Lawbook $14.95
___ Complete Lost In Space $19.95	___ Cheers: Where Everybody Knows Your Name $14.95
___ ..doctor Who Encyclopedia: Baker $19.95	___ SNL! The World Of Saturday Night Live $14.95
___ Lost In Space Tribute Book $14.95	___ The Rockford Phile $14.95
___ Lost In Space With Irwin Allen $14.95	___ Encyclopedia Of Cartoon Superstars $14.95
___ Doctor Who: Baker Years $19.95	___ How To Create Animation $14.95
___ Doctor Who: Pertwee Years $19.95	___ How To Draw Art For Comic Books $14.95
___ Batmania Ii $14.95	___ King And Barker:an Illustrated Guide $14.95
___ The Green Hornet $14.95 ___ Special Edition $16.95	___ King And Barker: An Illustrated Guide II $14.95

100% Satisfaction Guaranteed.

We value your support. You will receive a full refund as long as the copy of the book you are not happy with is received back by us in reasonable condition. No questions asked, except we would like to know how we failed you. Refunds and credits are given as soon as we receive back the item you do not want.

NAME:_____

STREET:_____

CITY:_____

STATE:_____

ZIP:_____

TOTAL:_____ SHIPPING_____

NG Crew

SEND TO: Couch Potato, Inc. 5715 N. Balsam Rd., Las Vegas, NV 89130

TREK

THE NEXT GENERATION CREW BOOK

James Van Hise

OTHER PIONEER BOOKS

•FISTS OF FURY: THE FILMS OF BRUCE LEE
Written by Edward Gross. March, 1990. $14.95, ISBN #1-55698-233-X
•WHO WAS THAT MASKED MAN? THE STORY OF THE LONE RANGER
Written by James Van Hise. March, 1990. $14.95, ISBN #1-55698-227-5
•PAUL MCCARTNEY: 20 YEARS ON HIS OWN
Written by Edward Gross. February, 1990. $9.95, ISBN #1-55698-263-1
•THE DARK SHADOWS TRIBUTE BOOK
Written by Edward Gross and James Van Hise. February, 1990. $14.95, ISBN#1-55698-234-8
•THE UNOFFICIAL TALE OF BEAUTY AND THE BEAST, 2nd Edition
Written by Edward Gross. $14.95, 164 pages, ISBN #1-55698-261-5
•TREK: THE LOST YEARS
Written by Edward Gross. $12.95, 128 pages, ISBN #1-55698-220-8
•THE TREK ENCYCLOPEDIA
Written by John Peel. $19.95, 368 pages, ISBN#1-55698-205-4
•HOW TO DRAW ART FOR COMIC BOOKS
Written by James Van Hise. $14.95, 160 pages, ISBN#1-55698-254-2
•THE TREK CREW BOOK
Written by James Van Hise. $9.95, 112 pages, ISBN#1-55698-256-9
•BATMANIA
Written by James Van Hise. $14.95, 176 pages, ISBN#1-55698-252-6
•GUNSMOKE
Written by John Peel. $14.95, 204 pages, ISBN#1-55698-221-6
•ELVIS-THE MOVIES: THE MAGIC LIVES ON
Written by Hal Schuster. $14.95, ISBN#1-55698-223-2
•STILL ODD AFTER ALL THESE YEARS: ODD COUPLE COMPANION.
Written by Edward Gross. $12.95, 132 pages, ISBN#1-55698-224-0
•SECRET FILE: THE UNOFFICIAL MAKING OF A WISEGUY
Written by Edward Gross. $14.95, 164 pages, ISBN#1-55698-261-5

Publisher Hal Schuster
Editor David Lessnick
Designer Malrie Gregg

Library of Congress Cataloging-in-Publication Data
James Van Hise, 1949—
Trek The Next Generation Crew Book

1. Trek The Next Generation Crew Book (television)
I. Title

Published by Pioneer Books, Inc., 5715 N. Balsam Rd., Las Vegas, NV, 89130.

First Printing, 1993